The Leadership Advantage

The Leadership Advantage

How the Best Companies Are
Developing Their Talent to
Pave the Way for Future Success

Robert M. Fulmer
Jared L. Bleak

⁴AMACOM

American Management Association
New York • Atlanta • Brussels • Chicago • Mexico City • San Francisco
Shanghai • Tokyo • Toronto • Washington, D.C.

Special discounts on bulk quantities of AMACOM books are available to corporations, professional associations, and other organizations. For details, contact Special Sales Department, AMACOM, a division of American Management Association, 1601 Broadway, New York, NY 10019.
Tel: 212-903-8316. Fax: 212-903-8083.
E-mail: specialsls@amanet.org
Website: www.amacombooks.org/go/specialsales
To view all AMACOM titles go to: www.amacombooks.org

This publication is designed to provide accurate and authoritative information in regard to the subject matter covered. It is sold with the understanding that the publisher is not engaged in rendering legal, accounting, or other professional service. If legal advice or other expert assistance is required, the services of a competent professional person should be sought.

Library of Congress Cataloging-in-Publication Data

Fulmer, Robert M.
    The leadership advantage : how the best companies are developing their talent to pave the way for future success / Robert M. Fulmer, Jared L. Bleak.
        p.   cm.
    Includes bibliographical references and index.
    ISBN-13: 978-0-8144-0925-1 (hardcover)
    ISBN-10: 0-8144-0925-3 (hardcover)
    1. Executives—Training of.   2. Executives—Training of—Case studies.   3. Leadership.   4. Organizational learning.   5. Success in business.   I. Bleak, Jared L.   II. Title.

HD30.4.F83   2007
658.4'092—dc22   *2007011453*

Printing number

10   9   8   7   6   5   4   3   2   1

Contents

Preface

Change continues to be the major constant in the competitive global business environment. The challenge of keeping up with, or leading, technology has never been more daunting. Competition is coming from new and unanticipated sources. But perhaps the most critical change facing senior executives in global organizations today is the task of preparing a new generation of leaders who will extend the strategic reach of the organizations they lead. Being "built to last" requires constant renewal. This renewal is typically based on leaders' continuing to develop themselves and their successor generation.

Leadership and learning play a critical role in enabling organizational growth and transformation. Today's and tomorrow's leaders must be flexible, collaborative, able to leverage subject-matter expertise, and willing to continue learning. Learning organizations must be able to support leaders as they develop the aforementioned characteristics.

There are real opportunities for synergies between the current generation of top executives and the leaders who will succeed them. While leveraging leadership-development programs to achieve their own objectives, top executives can also contribute to the development of younger managers. By serving as teachers and role models, these top executives provide direction and insight into their strategic goals and help to ensure that the company's leadership strategy and development programs support the strategic needs of the business, today and tomorrow. The learning organization, in turn, benefits from greater insight into its business challenges while simultaneously providing increasingly targeted development programs that result in improved organizational capability.

Organizational capability does not come just from a collection of talented and individually competent people but also stems from the organization's collective ability to act as one in meeting its strategy. Therefore, closing gaps in the organization's ability to execute its strategic initiatives is distinct from closing gaps in an individual's competency. An organizational capability focus shifts developmental priorities and requires coordination of initiatives (e.g., job rotations, special projects, formal training, mentoring, assessment, coaching, and action learning) among people within a group and across groups. It also recognizes that organizational capability requires developing the *collective* capabilities of various groups and teams within the organization. Other ways of increasing organizational capability include the improvement of infrastructure to support the desired capability, greater alignment with strategy, the improvement of employee skills and technical expertise, and change in the organizational culture. The ability of groups and teams to work together effectively requires more than the right combination of individual competencies. It requires its own attention in building organizational capability.

The American Productivity and Quality Center (APQC), the Center for Creative Leadership (CCL), and Duke Corporate Education (Duke CE) joined forces in 2006 to conduct a benchmarking study to gain a better understanding of how to elevate the importance of the leadership-development function as a must-have for executing strategy (not a nice-to-have for developing individuals). The research team also wanted to learn how a strategy for developing leaders and an integrated leadership-development architecture can contribute to business success. By gaining insights into the best approaches for evaluating leadership development, we hope to find ways of gaining success at the individual and organizational levels.

Study Scope

The objectives of this study were to:

▲ Discover best practices in tying leadership culture, values, practices, and development to business strategy

▲ Identify best practices for creating strategically relevant collective-learning opportunities

▲ Uncover architectures for integrating various development initiatives for maximum impact

▲ Understand how organizations use leadership development to support the execution of business strategy and how to meet long-term needs to develop individual competencies while also building immediately needed organizational capability to address business challenges

The organizations selected for deep, detailed study through structured data collection and site visits (also known as best-practice partners) demonstrate innovative performance in one or more of the study focus areas. The goal of the project was to examine organizations that excel in one or more aspects of the scope and determine the best practices from all the organizations studied. To achieve this goal, the APQC study team selected potential best-practice partners for study, based on a history of excellence and success in the scope areas. Project sponsors—organizations that sponsored the research, were interested in learning from the study's results, and participated in site visits and formal research—selected the final list of best-practice companies from the candidates. The project sponsors also served as a comparator group to the best-practice partners by participating in the survey that was administered. This comparison is made throughout the book.

Acknowledgments

We express our appreciation to the best-practice partner organizations and the specific individuals from each organization who were part of the study, including:

▲ Caterpillar: Chris Arvin, dean, College of Leadership; Deb Conklin, succession planning manager; Kim Converse, senior learning consultant; Pat Murphy, manager, succession management; Deb Nelson, senior learning consultant; Chris Schena, vice president, Motion and Power Control Division; Mary Seely, human resource manager, North American Commercial Division.

▲ Cisco Systems: Lisa Cavallaro, manager, WW Leadership Development; Beryl Fajardo, manager, WW Leadership Development; Pat Keating, director, WW Leadership Development; Patrick Tse, manager, WW Leadership Development, who also reviewed Cisco's material for this book.

▲ PepsiCo: Allan Church, vice president, Organization & Management Development; Paul Russell, vice president, Executive Learning & Development.

▲ PricewaterhouseCoopers: Jim Klee, chief operating officer, Learning & Education; Kathryn Kavanagh, managing director, Partner Leadership Development, Learning & Education; Dan Goepp, managing director, Assurance Practice, Learning & Education; Luciana Duarte, director, Learning and Education.

▲ Washington Group International: Jennifer A. Large, vice president, Integrated Staffing and Talent Management; Stephen P. Muller, director, Employee Development; Larry L. Myers, senior vice president, Human Resources.

Of course, we are greatly indebted to our friends at the American Productivity and Quality Center (APQC) for their support in this and previous research projects. Their unique approach to benchmarking, staff support, and permission to use these data are all greatly appreciated. Special thanks go to Carla O'Dell, CEO; Darcy Lemons, project manager; Wesley Vestal, who helped launch the project; and Uchenna Conley, project analyst.

Finally, we appreciate greatly the help of our colleagues at Duke Corporate Education, including Gordon Armstrong, Stephanie Scott, Paul Baerman, and Molly Darnofal. We also are grateful for the insights of John Alexander, CEO of the Center for Creative Leadership (CCL), and Reich Hughes, Director of R&D for CCL.

PART I

Leadership Development as a Strategic Force

What We Have Learned About Strategic Leadership Development

Great leaders deliver great results. This is perhaps the most profound finding from research on leadership development over the past decade. This phenomenon has been clearly articulated by astute gurus and seen by forward-thinking CEOs as key to developing true competitive advantage. Truly, organizations with strong leaders and superior leadership-development strategies deliver better results. In short, developing great leaders delivers great results and is a key determinant of business success.

Of course, leadership has never been a simple proposition. Observers have, throughout history, wondered if there were enough capable leaders to manage the challenges facing all types of organizations. Today, business and government organizations face something of a "perfect storm" of problems that has profound implications for current and future leaders. Some of these problems are:

▲ Competition is now coming from unexpected quarters. Because the rules of the business game are changing with this competition, current leaders represent what businesses needed in the past, rather than what they need in the present or future.

▲ Owing to the increasing "war for talent" sown by competition, the talent pipeline often lacks sufficient numbers to replace leaders who will soon retire.

▲ The organization's expansion goals outstrip the amount of talent needed to support them.

▲ Globalization and increasing technological demands make the leader's job more difficult than ever.

▲ Problems with strategic direction, organizational alignment, and employee commitment continue to exist and are exacerbated in the current competitive environment.

▲ Human resources and those responsible for leadership development feel increased pressure to demonstrate value, particularly in terms of return on investment for leader development and other education and training initiatives.

▲ Leadership-development initiatives are not integrated with business needs, and consequently, are of questionable value to internal customers.

The "perfect storm" of organizational challenges and leadership pressures has prompted study after study in the hope of determining the key to survival. And in study after study, superior financial and organizational performance, as well as other forms of success, have been linked to leadership. This comes as no surprise to those who have worked with or for a great leader. Good results follow good leadership. We are motivated by good leadership, guided by good leadership, and even held accountable by good leadership. In fact, employees who are led by strong leaders are more satisfied, engaged, and loyal than employees who follow weak leaders.[1] Most of all, we are often developed into good leaders ourselves as a result of being taught by and following the example of leaders who were role models, mentors, and teachers.

These findings have been confirmed across different dimensions of leadership development. (See Figure 1.1 for a list of significant studies on strategic leadership development that also appear in the references section.) For instance, in 2004, the Corporate Leadership Council found that organizations with strong leadership bench strength have approximately 10 percent higher total shareholder return than their weaker peers. Similarly, companies with above-average

Figure 1.1. Significant research used to frame strategic leadership-development project.

"Leadership Forecast: 2003–2004," by Paul Bernthal and Richard S. Wellins.

"Executive Development Trends 2000," by James Bolt.

"Executive Development Trends 2004: Filling the Talent Gap," by James Bolt.

"Executive Education: Evaluating the Return on Investment, Findings from the U.S.: An Appendix to the May 2005 Report," by Kate Charlton.

"Next Generation HR Practices," by Robert M. Fulmer.

"Strategic Human Resource Development," by Robert M. Fulmer.

"Developing Leaders: How Winning Companies Keep on Winning," by Robert M. Fulmer, Philip A. Gibbs, and Marshall Goldsmith.

The Leadership Investment: How the World's Best Organizations Gain Strategic Advantage Through Leadership Development, by Robert M. Fulmer and Marshall Goldsmith.

"How to Grow Great Leaders," by Douglas A. Ready.

"How the Top 20 Companies Grow Great Leaders," by Michelle Salob and Shelli Greenslade, Hewitt Associates.

"Current Challenges in Leadership Development," by Scott Saslow.

"Transforming Corporate Leadership: Best Practices in Executive Education," by Scott Saslow.

"Sixth Annual Benchmarking Report," Corporate University Xchange, 2004.

Note: Publishing details are provided in the references section.

financial returns have more comprehensive succession planning processes and are more committed to developing future leaders.[2]

Five Guiding Principles for Leadership Development

What evokes these results? Previous research has yielded five guiding principles for leadership development in general. Companies have shown that by following these principles they can effectively improve their leadership-development results and streamline their organizations' focus on leadership development.

1. Start at the top.
2. Link leadership development directly to the business and deliver results.
3. Build an integrated leadership strategy.
4. Drive consistency in the execution of leadership programs and practices.
5. Hold leaders and the organization accountable for results, both developmental and business.

The research has shown that individually each of these principles will yield positive results; however, practiced together, they can propel an organization to new heights in leadership development. Let's discuss each in depth.

1. Start at the Top

The engagement of CEO support for leadership development is often what separates the top-performing companies from the rest. In a study of the top twenty companies for leaders, Hewitt Associates found that 100 percent of these companies involved the CEO in leadership development and many initiatives were sponsored directly by the chief executive, compared with 65 percent of other companies studied. Similarly, board-level involvement makes a difference in leadership development. A majority of top companies (65 percent) involved the board in leadership-development activities and processes, compared with only 31 percent of other companies.

However, involvement of senior leaders doesn't stop with endorsing and sponsoring programs. A current trend is to use top leaders as teachers in developmental programs as well as coaches and mentors to high potentials. In fact, 75 percent of leading learning and development organizations identified the use of senior executives as faculty as the predominant trend in the near term. In addition, just over half of the respondents from this same group noted that the use of executives as coaches would be a significant trend.

Crotonville, the internal training and development department of General Electric (GE), became a household name because of the importance placed on it by CEO Jack Welch. And not only did Welch espouse the strategic importance of learning and development, but also he modeled it by staying deeply involved in the company's efforts. Other examples of executive involvement at the very highest levels include PepsiCo's Roger Enrico in the past decade and Caterpillar's Jim Owens in the current decade. Both of the latter have been intimately involved in their organization's leadership-development strategies and have seen great results from their efforts.

Using senior executives as teachers and coaches can also be a risky proposition. If training time is not set aside to improve their teaching and coaching skills, senior executives often become frustrated with their lack of success and the inherent difficulty of teaching. In the process, some developing leaders grow disillusioned. Giving presentations, which many executives do well, is different from teaching. Executives frequently need to be taught to become effective teachers.

2. Link Leadership Development Directly to the Business and Deliver Results

Keeping personal development in mind, organizations should emphasize business objectives when crafting leadership-development plans. Hewitt found that the top 20 companies in the United States in leadership development closely linked development strategies with business strategies. This linkage was established despite the temptation to build development plans composed primarily of best practices from other companies or heralded in benchmark studies and training magazines. Indeed, alignment between leadership-development strategy and business strategy often won out over a hodgepodge of benchmark programs.

As they grow more attuned to and concerned with measuring the impact of leadership-development activities on business success, companies are developing better methods of assessing this impact. For instance, 70 percent of corporate universities measure the impact of education on product or service quality, as well as customer service. And 59 percent measure reduced operating costs as a result of leadership development. Other measures include increased revenues (51 percent), improved sales efficiency (49 percent), and increased profits (48 percent).[3] Yet even with solid measures available, less than one company in five currently tracks business results from leadership-development activities, as compared to over three in four companies that measure participant satisfaction and learning.

Challenges associated with measuring the business impact of leadership development help to explain the reluctance to track such results. These challenges include creating a common language that defines value, gaining access to appropriate business data, and finding matched samples to contrast with leadership-development participants.

3. Build an Integrated Leadership Strategy

Perhaps the most significant, overarching trend in leadership development stems from the pressure to organize development activities and initiatives into an integrated strategy. In a 2004 study, 69 percent of respondents noted that the "creation of an integrated strategy and system for all executive development" was the leading priority of their learning and development organizations. These results mirrored those of a study conducted in 2000.[4]

Many learning and development organizations see leadership development as a set of puzzle pieces representing initiatives and programs that somehow fit together but don't seem to ever come together in the right way. These pieces include competency models, 360-degree and other assessments, developmental job rotations, experiential and action learning, talent management, succession planning, rewards and recognition, and coaching and mentoring. A leadership-development architecture can bring these often disjointed elements together into a consummate whole that has a greater chance of delivering real results. However, this architecture must be integrated with and linked to the strategy and needs of the business in order to increase the impact. It must also be communicated widely within the organization to engender support.[5]

4. Drive Consistency in the Execution of Leadership Programs and Practices

The best companies consistently execute strategies that make for good leadership development. They create enterprise-wide standards, practices, and metrics for leadership; they cascade programs and processes down through the organization to improve impact and drive cultural change; they illustrate flexibility in centralized leadership-development programs in order to address specific business needs; and they customize developmental solutions for business units in order to better ensure support and engagement by senior management.

An important leverage point in leadership-development efforts is the high-potential leader population within companies. Indeed, accelerating the development of high potentials was listed as a key objective by 62 percent of learning and development professionals. However, even with this objective in mind, 46 percent of companies have no systemic process for identifying and developing candidates for key leadership positions, including high potentials. And 37 percent of companies see their ability to identify leadership potential as a serious weakness. Among the top companies in leadership development, 95 percent identify high potentials as compared to 77 percent of other companies. Additionally, 68 percent inform those high potentials of their status and 72 percent track their progress and turnover. Even greater differentiation in the development of high potentials can be seen in the techniques and methods used by the top companies in leadership development. Ninety-five percent of top companies provide increased access to senior leaders for their high potentials, as compared to 45 percent of other companies. Similarly, top companies provide internal training (90 percent vs. 51 percent), developmental assignments (89 percent vs. 43 percent), and mentoring and coaching (58 percent vs. 24 percent) at a much higher rate than did companies not considered benchmarks for leadership development.[6]

In the absence of an effective succession-management strategy and process, a company's efforts to create a good high-potential development program can end in frustration. Overall, half of internal candidates selected for leadership positions fail when there is no succession-management system in place. And if they had the opportunity, organizations would rehire only 62 percent of their executives.[7] To increase the odds of success, an effective succession-management process should include visible support by senior management and line leaders who identify and develop succession candidates, a time frame for achieving planned development actions, flexibility to change in response to strategic needs or competitive pressures, and the sharing of information with candidates.

5. Hold Leaders and the Organization Accountable for Results, Both Developmental and Business

Holding people and the organization accountable for development efforts is a trend that continues to gain momentum, especially in an increasingly competitive environment where any investment or outlay is carefully considered and monitored for a return. In fact, 52 percent of learning and development professionals plan to use systematic measurement and evaluation to measure the impact of their development efforts.

Best-practice firms anchor their leadership-development efforts with lean competency models tied to performance and reward systems. In recent years, top companies have begun to integrate their competencies into succession planning (100 percent of top companies vs. 78 percent of others) and make the competencies a baseline for identifying and then developing high potentials. In the top quartile of leadership-development companies identified by Hewitt Associates, a human resources consulting company, metrics were integrated with succession planning 71 percent of the time, versus only 45 percent of the time in companies in the bottom quartile. These top companies also more fully integrated competency measures into formulas for base pay (60 percent vs. 30 percent), annual incentives (60 percent vs. 31 percent), and long-term incentives (65 percent vs. 23 percent).

Top leadership-development companies also use competencies as metrics in the performance-management processes. These competencies are established as behavioral standards for leaders and managers. Pay is influenced according to performance against these standards. Of course, in order to be useful, competencies must be clear, easily understandable, and readily observable.

Many companies do not measure the impact of learning and development as they should. In one 2004 study, 63 percent of European multinational organizations reported never measuring return on investment in learning and development, even though these same firms reported that the importance being placed on learning and development within the organization was higher than ever before.[8] There is clearly more work to be done in holding people and organizations accountable for learning and development results.

Research Background: Meeting Current Challenges

Inspired by the knowledge that today's organizations are being challenged to develop their people as never before, the American Productivity and Quality Center (APQC), the Center for Creative Leadership (CCL), and Duke Corporate Education (Duke CE) decided to collaborate on a benchmarking study to build on what was already known and to stimulate awareness of current best practices in aligning development and implementation strategies with organizational goals. The remainder of this chapter introduces the highlights of our research on strategic leadership development. It also outlines what we believe to be "best practices" in the broader leadership-development arena.

The best-practice companies selected for further research were subjected to deep, detailed study through structured data collection and site visits. The goals of the research were to examine these organizations and determine best practices in the following areas:

▲ Tying leadership culture, values, practices, and development to business strategy

▲ Creating strategically relevant collective-learning opportunities

▲ Integrating various development initiatives for maximum impact into an overall leadership-development architecture

▲ Using leadership development to support the execution of business strategy

▲ Meeting long-term needs for developing individual competencies while also building immediately needed organizational capability to address business challenges

Building the Leadership Advantage

High potentials in many leadership-development programs will be at the very top of their organizations in ten to fifteen years. The challenge for organizations in developing a leadership advantage thus becomes a goal with a long-term horizon and return. The results of our research confirm, in many important ways, much of the research conducted on leadership development to date while also offering important additions and clarifications. Our results fall into four broad themes:

1. Making leadership development a strategic lever

2. Building an aligned architecture for strategic leadership development

3. Implementing successful strategic leadership development

4. Evaluating success

Subsequent chapters in the book correspond to each theme, with Chapters 4 and 5 covering the third theme. Within these broad themes, we have broken down the key findings of our research into fifteen more specific messages. Each of these concepts is previewed below as a prelude to a more thorough discussion.

Making Leadership Development a Strategic Lever (Chapter 2)

Organizations experience major change events leading to profound teachable moments. Much has been written about the importance of providing developmental opportunities for individuals at appropriate "teachable moments." There is ample evidence to suggest that managers benefit more from educational experiences that occur "just in time" to apply new knowledge, rather than "just in case" they eventually need a new set of skills. These teachable moments often occur when individuals have just been asked to change their roles—for example, become managers rather than individual contributors, become managers of managers, or become general managers with overall operational responsibility for a business unit.

Similarly, organizations seem to have moments when the development and articulation of a leadership strategy are especially appropriate. In our research, it appears that these opportunities generally occur when there is a new CEO who wishes to align the organization around a new strategy, when two organizations have merged, or when there is a significant organizational crisis. For example, when Jim Owens became CEO of Caterpillar, he encouraged the Leadership College of Caterpillar University to create a Leadership Quest program for the corporation's high potentials.

In 2002, Washington Group International (Washington Group), an engineering, construction, and management solutions firm, emerged from Chapter 11 with a four-person office of the chairman headed by Stephen Hanks as CEO and a new threefold mission statement that identified people and their development, as well as profitability and performance, as top priorities. According to Hanks, "the company that develops talent the fastest will take the hill."

Each best-practice company we studied used a key organizational transition to develop, articulate, and align a new leadership strategy with the strategic direction of the company. These transitions became teachable moments for the organization and formed crucial starting points for achieving excellence in leader development.

Winning organizations build a strong linkage between business strategy and leadership-development strategy. A direct link between a leadership-development strategy and corporate strategy provides great benefit to an organization and its employees. Alignment with corporate strategy is a key element of successful leadership development. Organizations that realize this establish a leader-development philosophy that permeates all levels of the organization and is meaningful to all employees.

This was clearly evident in the best-practice companies we studied. All of these organizations tied leadership development to corporate planning as well as business strategy. At Caterpillar, alignment is achieved by receiving input from the executive office, business units, and process owners of the critical success factors. To further embed leadership development in the business strategy, Caterpillar established metrics to connect leadership to the business. Similarly, PricewaterhouseCoopers (PwC) links development activities to its strategy of becoming the "distinctive firm." Successful programs at PwC are designed to reinforce corporate strategy, thus ensuring linkage and success.

As these short examples show, each best-practice company works hard to ensure that emerging leaders are prepared for the future and its challenges, rather than hindered by the past.

Executives use leadership development as a powerful tool to formulate, translate, and communicate strategy. While education is a relatively small portion of the entire developmental process for leaders, carefully crafted learning initiatives allow an organization to garner input from employees throughout the organization. These initiatives also help to effectively communicate the reasons for and implications of corporate strategy to managers who will need to translate the strategy for employees so they understand their roles in implementing the strategy.

Various studies have concluded that 60 to 70 percent of all strategies fail to be successfully implemented. Our best-practice partners seem to have discovered that one way to beat these odds is to ensure that all employees in the organization understand the strategy, the reasons for it, and their roles in implementing the strategy. These companies also understand that developmental activities can be an effective means of sharing information and providing tools for successful implementation.

Lean competency models and values are the foundations of strategic leadership development. A simple leadership model with a concise statement of values serves as an important point of focus in leadership development. None of the best-practice partners studied had a scientifically valid competency model; most had created their own model or had adapted it from a set of competencies developed by an outside firm.

In contrast, the best-practice companies in our research kept their values and competencies simple and straightforward, understanding that competencies should apply at all levels in an organization and directly lead to better performance.

Building an Aligned Architecture for Strategic Leadership Development (Chapter 3)

Strategic leadership development depends on a partnership between senior executives and multiple human resource systems. Senior executive support, usually starting with the CEO, is vital for success in strategic leadership development. Yet, even the most effective CEO cannot ensure success without the involvement of the entire human resource system. Conversely, training and education professionals will not be successful unless they collaborate with their colleagues in line positions and in other human resource specialties.

For example, within Cisco Systems's HR function, the organization's Worldwide Leadership Development group works with company leaders to identify candidates for its leadership-development programs. Executives then help to design the programs, ensuring that the programs meet business needs and align with strategy. For example, at Washington Group, corporate leaders and its six business units share responsibility for leadership development. The integrated staffing and talent-management function is responsible for the design, development, implementation, and maintenance of the programs, while the office of the chairman reviews, approves, and provides feedback on moving forward with development. The fourteen-member senior-executive leadership team meets regularly to discuss leadership development.

As leadership development increases in importance, partnerships with executives and HR will have to continue to be strengthened in order for these efforts to succeed.

Strategic human resource development is a key part of the corporate planning cycle. Another test for determining if developing leaders is a strategic priority for a company is to see if there is a human resource development (HRD) component to the planning cycle. The best-practice companies in this study make people planning, as well as succession planning, something that every key executive is expected to address in concert with his or her human resource partners and the immediate supervisor. In other words, it makes sense to consider which key players are expected to implement the strategy and what assistance they will need to enhance the probability of success.

For example, Washington Group leverages its annual strategic and business planning sessions to discuss employee development and leadership-development needs. Similarly, PepsiCo's career-growth model aligns with the organization's annual operating calendar. These two examples lead to a strong conclusion that successful development of leaders requires a strategic alignment of planning and all human resource systems.

Human resource development can win the support of top management by involving them in strategic learning initiatives and by understanding the business. Most of the exemplars in this study have a high degree of executive involvement in the delivery of key corporate programs. Similarly, executive involvement in program design can ensure that program content addresses topics of genuine concern to key constituencies and contributes to higher levels of support for the ongoing initiative.

At Cisco Systems, each program has an established cross-functional executive steering committee that ensures linkage between the program and the business. The business leaders on these steering committees help drive the design of the programs and recruit appropriate executives for the classrooms. During the design phase of a program, the steering committees meet often. In addition, the programs employ the role of executive faculty—people who bring participants a strategic perspective.

A Board of Governors for Caterpillar University, which includes the CEO and other senior executives, approves learning budgets and priorities as well as determines policy. Advisory boards for each college within Caterpillar University include senior leaders from business or user groups. These boards are diverse in terms of geography and subject-matter expertise, and they include members from most of Caterpillar's business units.

Although it is important to involve line executives with a deep understanding of the business challenges facing an organization in program design, executive involvement is not sufficient to ensure a program's success. Successful HRD partners must understand the business in addition to recognizing leading-edge leadership concepts.

Leaders who teach are more effective than those who tell. One of the surprising findings of this project was the degree to which senior executives practice the concept of leading by teaching. At PepsiCo, Paul Russell, vice president of executive learning & development, speaks of "the magic of leaders developing leaders." According to Russell, the missing adult-learning principle is that "people learn best when they get to learn from someone they really want to learn from." Russell notes that "at PepsiCo, the 'teachers' our executives want to learn from are our own senior leaders. They are world class, widely respected, and have proven that they can do it here!"

At PepsiCo, senior executives are asked to share their personal perspectives, as well as build participant confidence and skills while demonstrating support for their growth. Of equal importance, senior leaders elicit greater teamwork from participants and get to know key young leaders while developing more loyalty, motivation, and productivity among employees and creating greater alignment around vision and key strategic initiatives. PepsiCo leaders are encouraged to think of learning as an important arrow in their quiver for helping to drive change. At PepsiCo, learning becomes something to live, not just another thing to endorse.

Implementing Successful Strategic Leadership Development (Chapters 4 and 5)

Human resource development owns the process and maintains strategic control. A somewhat surprising finding was the degree to which the best-practice partners maintained control of the design and delivery of their leadership-development programs while leveraging input from trusted outside partners or advisers. All had relatively small staffs for the HRD function yet had delegated relatively little to outsiders.

As a professional-services firm, PwC has high levels of involvement with outside professionals. Consequently, the firm believes that its partners' time can be better spent helping their own clients than trying to become experts in HRD. PwC's Learning and Education Group has 250 employees; however, most of these employees are involved in technical and professional learning. A very small group, concerned with leadership and partner development, is totally involved in every aspect of its programs but relies on external vendors for some assistance in design and much help in delivery.

Washington Group's leadership development is coordinated by the firm's integrated staffing and talent-management function (part of the human resources organization). It uses outside consultants to a limited degree and relies on its senior leaders to do much of the actual instruction. It also enlists retired executives who know the firm, its culture, and the industry. Caterpillar worked closely with the Hay Group to develop its Making Great Leaders program and leadership framework. It also asked Duke CE to facilitate the Leadership Quest program and to coach officers in planning their sessions for the course.

Lean human resource departments leverage their talents by partnering with outside experts. Although leadership development remains firmly under the control of the company, the lean corporate staffs of the best-practice companies leverage their time and talents with the judicious use of outside expertise. Because of the emphasis on knowing the business and on lead staffing, most of the best-practice companies involved outside firms or specialists in both the design and delivery of their learning initiatives. However, no matter how busy they are, these companies never completely relinquish the challenge of design and delivery to others.

In none of the best-practice companies is leadership development an island. There is a growing trend toward partnership and alignment with succession planning and performance management, as well as other HR activities. Fortunately, the leadership-development silo seems to have been punctured and is hardly recognizable among the best-practice companies in this study.

Integration of leadership development with other talent-management systems creates synergies. Organizations committed to leadership development understand its relationship with other talent-management systems and practices. The best-practice partners incorporate their leadership-development programs with other processes such as performance reviews, management development, and succession planning.

The best-practice partners have invested heavily in their people. In so doing, they have inevitably integrated leadership development with other talent-management systems in order to receive the maximum benefit. Washington Group is such a strong proponent of this mindset that it integrates every aspect of talent management. This process begins with establishing a vision of what positions will need to be filled and then moves to forecasting, identifying, and preparing candidates. Subsequently, development plans are carefully crafted for each employee. An overall employee-development strategic plan then feeds the succession-planning process, which in turn is used in the leadership-development program.

Cisco uses executive coaches to accelerate development as part of its high-potential program. High potentials are paired with an external executive coach for a year. Although the coach is an external resource, he or she is fully trained and knowledgeable in "the Cisco way" prior to the assignment.

Corporate learning initiatives tend to focus on high potentials. Substantial organizational impact can be gained by involving small numbers of people with high potential, who will return to their regular jobs and translate their learning to others in various operations, via educational initiatives. Similarly, many key corporate programs can be adapted by business groups that wish to provide a similar experience for their key people that aligns with the corporate emphasis.

Although PwC designed its PwC University experience for 2,000 U.S. partners, and Caterpillar involved all leaders in its 2005 strategy rollout, most key corporate initiatives in our study were focused on high potentials. Caterpillar's Leadership Quest involves approximately fifty key midlevel leaders per year. PepsiCo's CEO program involves approximately forty high potentials each year. Washington Group's Leadership Excellence and Performance (LEAP) project began in 2002 and had graduated forty-eight participants by mid-2006. Cisco's Executive Leader Program focuses on the company's strategic intent and serves approximately forty top leaders annually. This latter program was designed for employees who are currently filling or have been newly promoted to the role of vice president.

Evaluating Success in Strategic Leadership Development (Chapter 6)

Developing people is a growing measure of executive success. Best-practice partners take the development of people very seriously. They seem to believe that financial results are a lagging indicator of organizational success while people development is a leading indicator. Consequently, people development is becoming an important part of the assessment of executive performance.

PepsiCo has historically allocated two-thirds of incentive compensation for achieving business results and one-third of compensation

for achieving people results. In 2007, PepsiCo moved to an equal allocation of incentive compensation for both business and people results in order to reinforce the importance of developing talent and
building an inclusive environment. PepsiCo also uses the results from
its semiannual organizational-health survey and 360-degree feedback
process as part of the performance-review process.

Caterpillar found that its managers needed improvement in the
legacy (developmental) set of behaviors. Consequently, the company
has begun to focus on legacy in learning programs and in performance assessment.

*Return on learning is increasingly measured by corporate
success rather than by individual performance.* The standard in
assessing corporate training programs and initiatives has been the
Kirkpatrick and Phillips models of evaluation.[9] Each of the best-
practice partners were familiar with and used parts of these models
but also pushed on to think about measuring the results of learning
in new and innovative ways.

Because Caterpillar University was established during an economic recession, the company may have felt pressured to establish
the value proposition for learning early in its history. As part of this
process, Caterpillar University created a document called the "Business of Learning," in which each college developed a value proposition for key initiatives based on net benefits, ROI, and other
standards. This document later evolved into the "Enterprise Learning
Plan," a 161-page document that discussed the current state of learning at Caterpillar and articulated the value proposition for learning.
The development of the "Enterprise Learning Plan" was then followed by seven detailed ROI studies. These leveraged focus groups,
surveys, and in-depth discussions with participants. They identified
the intangible and dollar benefits, costs, and ROI of educational initiatives. Having already established the value proposition for learning,
Caterpillar doesn't need to repeat this process for subsequent itera-
tions of a program. The company is beginning to speak about "return
on learning" (ROL) rather than the more formalized process for ROI.

PepsiCo doesn't attempt to measure the value created by an educational program, but its CEO attends each of the major high-potential programs and serves as the primary facilitator. Since the CEO is intensely involved with program design and delivery, ratings are less of a problem for her because of her familiarity with the program and its participants. At the end of each program, each participant is asked to send her an e-mail indicating what he or she will be doing differently as a result of attending the session. Participants are also asked to send the CEO another e-mail six months later, reporting on how thoroughly they have met their commitments.

Cisco collects both quantitative and qualitative measures of the value of learning. The company's Worldwide Leadership Development group has a formal system for measuring the outcomes of leadership-development strategy. Examples of metrics include "price range for a one-week course," "customer satisfaction scores," "percentage of program alumni who have used what they have learned in their jobs and had a positive impact," and "percentage of learners who stay with the company." The team concentrates on metrics, showing the application of learning to jobs and changes in business results. One example of measurement is the retention percentage for employees going through the programs as compared to the general employee population. This retention percentage has been quite favorable for Cisco—approximately 93 percent across the organization.

Successful programs are a process rather than an event. In past years, corporate education programs have been a disconnected series of events. Today, they are typically part of an integrated career-development plan that is tied to strategic objectives with specific and actionable objectives. These programs are seldom one-week, discrete events and, rather, often include team or individual applications.

The Cisco Leadership Series operates in a three-phase structure that facilitates employees' ability to put learning into action. The series reflects an events-to-process model. Employees involved in the various programs progress through each phase: preparation, residential, and application on the job. Although the residential portion of Cisco's programs may last only five days, the participants are involved in the learning process for eight to ten months.

Caterpillar's core leadership programs leverage key transition points in its leaders' careers. These transitions take place as individuals move from supervisor (i.e., frontline leader), to manager (leader of leaders), to department head, and finally to executive. A person's movement through these programs and his or her transitions are all part of the developmental journey at Caterpillar. Also, these programs are being built on one another in a building-block fashion. Underlying all of these programs is Caterpillar's foundational Making Great Leaders program.

Getting to Great Results: Summary

No business strategy is good enough to succeed without strong leadership. And this strong leadership has been shown to be the essence of exceptional organizational performance. Leadership and learning should play critical roles in enabling organizational growth and transformation. Today's leaders must be flexible, collaborative, able to leverage subject-matter expertise, and willing to continue their learning journey.

The best-practice companies in our study understand these principles well and have created best-in-class leadership-development strategies, practices, and measures that contribute to overall financial and strategic success. They know that great leaders deliver great results.

The next six chapters take a deeper look at the themes and principles we've just introduced. More in-depth results from the study will be given, and further connections will be drawn. After that are case studies from the best-practice companies that detail the systems and processes that have made them best-in-class for leadership development.

chapter 2

Making Leadership Development
a Strategic Lever

Have you ever lived in a city that had failed to do adequate planning for growth and development? With due respect to our friends at the American Productivity and Quality Center (APQC), we feel that Houston may be a prime example of this sort of failure. Beautiful buildings coexist with ramshackle structures. An upscale furniture store sits adjacent to a used-car lot. The net effect, in our opinion, is that Houston does not meet its potential for becoming a beautiful city. Although we are admittedly biased, we believe Santa Barbara is an example of success in urban development. The city took advantage of a 1925 earthquake to reinvent itself. With strong civic leadership provided by Pearl Chase and downtown merchants, the city established and enforced strong zoning requirements that demanded consistency in architecture and created a harmonious appearance in the business areas of the city.

In recent years, many human resource (HR) and human resource development (HRD) departments have grown haphazardly, without regard for an overall plan or strategy. For example, typically one system was introduced a decade ago and seemed to work reasonably well, yet was not fully integrated with newer systems. This led to inconsistencies and ultimately to each component of HR having a manager who may be more interested in the elegance of his or her system than in how it connected to other parts of the company. One of the major shifts in human resources during the past decade or two has been away from almost-independent components and to a consciously articulated leadership and human-resource strategy that is integrated and aligned with overall corporate strategy. However, this transition is far from complete in many firms.

Just as Houston has attractive neighborhoods that fail to come together to create a cohesive urban environment, so some organizations have pockets of excellence that fail to be integrated into a unified whole. Excellent educational programs that are not part of the strategic direction of the firm or that fail to support the business objectives of the organization reduce the overall potential of the group. Likewise, strategic goals that are not supported by reward and promotion policies are likely to be ignored.

Strong, aligned leadership is essential to business success. Sometimes a traumatic, or at least dramatic, event can lead to a conscious reinvention that moves an organization ahead on its path to greatness. But leadership is an essential element of the success of any strategic change effort. Indeed, no strategy is good enough to succeed without strong leadership.

The skills and abilities of effective leaders can be developed through many avenues, such as coaching, mentoring, exchange with peers, skill building, stretch assignments, and opportunities to practice. These skills and abilities are just as important as individual qualities such as emotional intelligence, self-motivation, and being results-oriented. Attempts to create change must be communicated by, and to, those who are most impacted by the change. And change cannot be sustained unless organizations engage in self-examination, revise their systems and processes, and open decision-making opportunities to potential leaders.

Knowledge-building strategies such as leadership-development programs give high potentials access to information and highlight areas and opportunities for improvement. But in order to develop leaders in organizations, resources must be invested in the following:

▲ Skills building so that high-potential employees are exposed to a vast array of opportunities and knowledge

▲ Relationship building among executives, managers, and employees to remove inherent barriers between levels within an organization

▲ Strategies to ensure relevance and applicability to business goals within an organization

Creating a leadership-development strategy takes time. To implement a leadership-development strategy that lasts, executives and managers must support the building of leadership skills, devise the programs so new leaders are continuously developed and involved, and change policy and program decision making to encourage employee participation. There is no cookie-cutter model for leadership development. However, through our best-practice research, we have identified world-class practices to help other organizations see opportunities to adapt, rather than to copy, these practices to fit their unique situations.

Leadership pathways are affected by the resources, history, relationships, and other attributes of both the individual and the organization. They must be designed and crafted to meet the needs of each organization's culture, values, business strategy, and potential leaders. Figure 2.1 identifies some typical concerns of business leaders and suggests some ways that human resources can address these issues.

Setting the Context for Leadership Strategy

Based on our experience in working with global firms, as well as our research on best-practice companies, we believe that the following

Figure 2.1. Business concerns and responses of human resources.

Business Concerns	HR's Responses
1. Our competition is coming at us from unexpected quarters.	We are forced to create new rules for the game.
2. Our company is facing rapid change.	We need to rethink the business and its capabilities.
3. Our L&D organization is feeling increased pressure to demonstrate value.	We need to connect leadership development in an integrated way to the business strategy—and get results.
4. Our line leaders need to build new competencies and behaviors.	We need to align people with the strategic priorities of their organizations.
5. Our HR community has to improve retention of key talent.	We must ensure succession planning works.
6. Our company does not have the management talent necessary to run the business in the future.	We need to develop it.

SOURCE: Duke Corporate Education, 2007.

seven principles set the context for creating a foundational strategy to develop better leaders for the present and the future.

1. *Start with the business—and know the desired results.* The creator of Sherlock Holmes, Sir Arthur Conan Doyle, began writing his mysteries by focusing on the last chapter. The mystery of great leadership development may be just this simple. When attempting to craft a leadership-development strategy, ask, "What is the business issue I wish to address, and what is the result that will let me know that my organization has been successful?" In other words, start with a strategic mission for leadership that supports the overall business strategy.

2. *Insist on a systemic, integrated approach.* A program is seldom the solution to any problem. Building an exciting program isn't easy, but it is much less challenging than laying down the fundamen-

tal experiences that help individuals move through their careers while also moving the organization toward its strategic goals. However challenging, creating an integrated approach is critical to an organization's success in developing its people.

3. *Think about building organizational capability, as well as individual leaders.* We believe that "management development" is dead among leading firms. Obviously, there is still a strategic need to develop individual leaders, but focusing on individual development apart from organizational strategy is simply providing competitors and headhunters with better people for recruitment. Action learning designed to address key organizational challenges can often provide solutions just as insightful and pragmatic as can outside consultants and it also contributes to the development of both the individual and the organization. Most important, however, is the capability that your best and brightest will have developed through the experience, and that you will have established the connection between individual and organizational development.

4. *Teach people to master (business) challenges, not competencies.* Competency models are important, but only if they address current and anticipated business issues. The key is for leaders to understand and master the business and for the competencies to align with that business.

5. *Measure outcomes and organizational impact regularly.* Chapter 6 addresses the challenge of assessment in greater detail. At this point, we simply want to emphasize that the plan for measurement of impact should be built into the original design of the business strategy.

6. *Request extensive C-suite and board participation.* Senior executives may believe that they are too busy for detailed participation in corporate learning initiatives. This study and previous research indicate that truly great leaders understand that there are few ways of leveraging their efforts and that sharing their visions is more effective than discussing their teachable point of view with the next generation of leaders.

7. *Keep the strategy flexible to allow the organization to respond to changes in the business.* Corporate HRD typically sets the agenda for major leadership programs. This department is responsible for ensuring that programs align with and support the overall corporate strategy. Divisional or strategic business-unit programs should connect with the corporate strategy, but they should also reflect environmental or competitive differences in their challenges. A program that was tremendously successful in its first iteration may become antiquated in a couple of years if it is not continually refined and improved.

An effective tool for involving senior line executives in program design and for enlisting their support is to ask about the major challenges that the key leaders of their business will need to address. Rather than soliciting topics to include in the educational program, ask line executives the following questions:

▲ What does your competition look like? How does this competition impact your need for change?

▲ Can you tell us about your company's, and top leaders', business challenges?

▲ Do you have the right people and capabilities to execute your strategy for future growth? If not, what are priority areas? Gaps?

▲ What leader competencies and behaviors are required to support the future direction of the organization? What obstacles inhibit organization growth today?

▲ How would you evaluate your current leadership pipeline? What needs to change?

▲ What programs and development experiences are best in class? What is missing?

▲ What else would you add to our discussion that "keeps you up at night"?

The rest of this chapter focuses on several aspects of developing a leadership strategy and builds on the aforementioned principles, such as acting on change, linking leadership development to corporate goals, communicating the leadership-development strategy, and building the strategy on a sound vision.

Key Findings on Strategic Design

Key findings on strategic design include organizations' use of "teachable moments," the linking of business and leadership-development strategies, the communication of strategy, and the identification and implementation of lean competency models.

Organizations Have Teachable Moments, Too

Key Finding 1. Organizations experience major change events leading to profound teachable moments.

Much has been written about the importance of providing developmental opportunities for individuals at the appropriate "teachable moment." There is ample evidence to suggest that executives and managers alike benefit more from educational experiences that occur "just in time" for them to apply their knowledge, rather than "just in case" they eventually need a new set of skills. These teachable moments often occur when individuals have just been asked to change their roles—for example, to become managers rather than individual contributors, to become managers of managers, or even to become general managers with overall operational responsibility for a business unit. In the case of executives, these moments often occur when they are asked to take the organization through a major transition, resulting in a shift in organizational identity or strategy. Another way to view this finding is to suggest that a new CEO or general manager who doesn't align the human resources systems with strategic initiatives is overlooking one of his or her most powerful implementation tools.

In this study, we found that best-practice partners use teachable moments to introduce new leadership-development initiatives to their respective organizations. Especially, organizations seem to have moments when the development and articulation of a leadership strategy are appropriate. These opportunities generally occur when there is a new CEO who wishes to align the organization around a new strategy, when two or more organizations have merged, or when there is a significant organizational crisis.

A recurring theme in our research findings was that each of the study's best-practice partners could name a specific situation in which it became clear to key line executives and senior human resources leaders that this was a strategic opportunity—a teachable moment. Each of the partners began the alignment of systems, along with the creation of specific leadership-development strategies, approximately three to five years before we started our research.

At the beginning of each partner's leadership-development story is a major change event, either a merger or an industry refocus. These change events led to the creation of a leadership-development mind-set that remains embedded in each organization today. At some point, each organization redirected its vision to focus on people. From this people focus emerged a leadership-development strategy that ensured the security, growth, and profitability of the organization well into the future.

For example, when Jim Owens became CEO of Caterpillar in 2004, one of his early decisions was to empower the College of Leadership within Caterpillar University to create a Leadership Quest program for the organization's highly promotable leaders. This program was built on an earlier initiative that Owens had been involved in as a young executive and also took inspiration from a program that had stressed the organization's leadership framework or competency model. The new initiative was intended to "give our next generation of leaders an infusion of 'yellow blood'" (a reference to the color of the organization's logo and many of its products).

As part of the Leadership Quest program, midlevel leaders were challenged to articulate what the strategy of Caterpillar should be in the year 2020. These recommendations were presented to the CEO during the program and circulated to the Strategic Planning Committee, which in October of 2005 articulated a new strategy called Vision 2020. Reflecting its namesake, this strategy predicted in detail the organization's needs through the year 2020. The fifteen-year outlook led executives to focus on the organization's future goals and to think about the requirements of future leaders. People were identified as a key element in this new strategy, an element that would help shape and support the strategic goals of the organization. The pyramid illustrated in Figure 2.2 has become a foundational graphic for conversations about strategy, operational planning, and leadership development at Caterpillar.

In order to create the culture needed to compete in the new environment for assurance, tax, and advisory services, in 2001, PricewaterhouseCoopers (PwC) articulated a set of corporate values, strategies, and leadership competencies that lead to the creation of a PwC University experience for all partners, along with a suite of other initiatives designed to enhance a culture totally aligned with the firm's strategy. The merger of Price Waterhouse and Coopers & Lybrand redirected PwC's energy, and a new vision surfaced to reflect the new

Figure 2.2. Caterpillar's enterprise strategy.

regulatory and competitive environment. The PwC vision was one of distinction and differentiation. In order to achieve the vision, leadership development became a central focus. PwC believes that the path to profitability starts with developing leaders who will be distinctive in the industry, ultimately leading to profitable growth.

In 2002, Washington Group emerged from financial restructuring with a new threefold mission statement that identified people as its first priority (see Figure 2.3). Washington Group, like the other best-practice partners in this study, approaches the future with the idea that developing its people will lead to sustainable long-term growth. As with the other partner organizations, Washington Group believes that a focus on people and on developing their talents will naturally enhance the organization's profitability.

PepsiCo's change event, which occurred in the mid-1990s, was a combination of mergers and new leadership. Today, PepsiCo has established a tradition of selecting new CEOs who use high-potential

Figure 2.3. Washington Group's threefold mission.

learning programs as a means of conveying both strategy and values to future corporate leaders. This tradition began with Roger Enrico, who as vice chairman of PepsiCo spent more than 120 days coaching and mentoring the next generation of PepsiCo leaders. With his vice president of executive development, Paul Russell, Enrico personally developed a program called Building the Business, and he led this program ten times in eighteen months.

When Steve Reinemund became CEO, he saw the opportunity to build capabilities in leaders for the organization's future and he developed his own approach to meeting this challenge. In October 2006, Indra Nooyi succeeded Reinemund as CEO. An experienced PepsiCo executive born and educated in India, she is evidence of the organization's commitment to diversity, internal development, and talent management. She is currently planning her unique approach to the next stage of the powerful PepsiCo tradition of CEO as "teacher in chief."

Cisco's teachable moment followed the dot-com crisis in the late 1990s. CEO John Chambers recognized the need for reinvigorated commitment to developing "emerging leaders" and "global leaders," and he brought Pat Keating, a former business school professor, to Cisco. As director of worldwide leadership education, Keating emphasizes the importance of maintaining a balance between growth and productivity. In Cisco's view, productivity requires collaboration and teamwork—two major thrusts of learning at Cisco.

Linking Business and Leadership-Development Strategies

Key Finding 2. Winning organizations build a strong linkage between business strategy and leadership-development strategy.

Many organizations develop an overarching corporate strategy and then build supporting strategies and systems around it to ensure that all programs are in alignment. There is a strong correlation between strategic alignment and the ultimate success of a strategy. In the case of a leadership-development strategy, the direct link between it and business strategy can provide great benefit to the organization and its employees. Organizations that realize the importance of this link establish a leadership-development philosophy that permeates all organizational levels and is applicable to all employees. This alignment embeds strategic leadership development in the DNA of the organization.

All of the study's partners indicated that leadership development is tied to their corporate planning process, yet this was true of only a third of the study sponsors, as shown in Figure 2.4. Indeed, the development and articulation of a leadership philosophy linking leadership to business strategy is a foundation of best practice and an important predictor of success. In our research, we found that alignment of strategies is key to ensuring that the leadership-development strategy is relevant to each business unit and, more important, to the overall business strategy.

Recently, Caterpillar realized that learning had to be linked to corporate strategy and critical success factors. At Caterpillar, alignment is achieved by receiving input from the executive office, business units,

Figure 2.4. To what extent are leadership-development programs at various levels aligned with the corporate/business strategy, with the desired corporate culture, and with each other?*

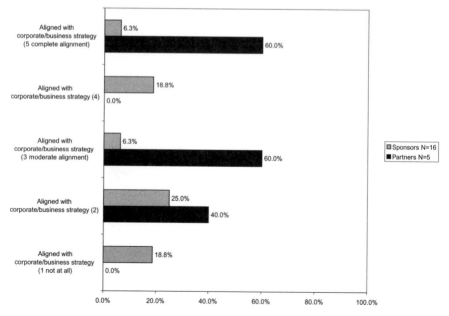

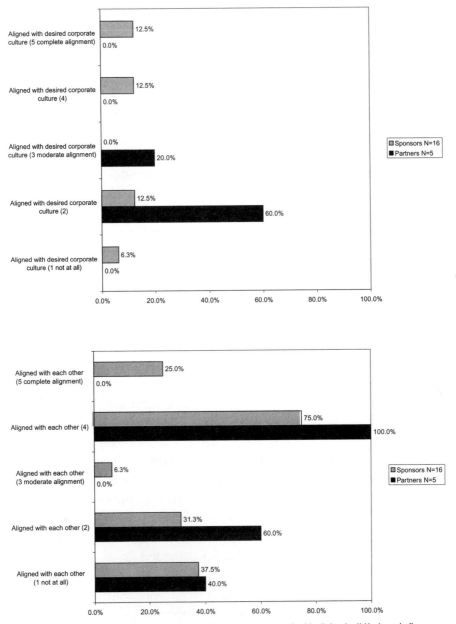

*Responses do not always add up to 100% as respondents were asked to "check all that apply."

and process owners of the critical success factors; however, the foundation of the alignment is the Enterprise Strategy (see Figure 2.2.). At Caterpillar, stakeholder inputs tie learning to business goals that eventually become the part of the Enterprise Learning Plan for the year. (See also the Caterpillar case study in Part II of this book.) To further embed leadership development in the business strategy, the company established metrics to connect leadership behavior to business success.

PricewaterhouseCoopers (PwC)'s leadership-development strategy is directly related to its "distinctive firm" strategy, which has business goals in three areas: client service, employee development, and quality work. These business goals and corporate strategy became the framework for the leadership strategy for PwC in North America. As a consequence, corporate and leadership strategies are linked. The leadership-development programs reinforce the corporate strategy and ensure success. Senior line executives sponsor the programs. Their sense of a program's value in achieving the firm's goals is a key factor in program success.

Washington Group also formally links its business strategy with its leadership-development strategy. It holds a series of strategic planning sessions during the year that encompass both the corporate strategy and the human resources strategy as they relate to business objectives. In these sessions, the organization's business strategy is reviewed and refined, and it becomes the basis for formal employee-development plans. In fact, all of these strategies guide leadership development. At Washington Group, the direct connection between business strategy and leadership-development strategy allows for employee development with near- and long-term action plans that ensure success in providing the leaders needed to confront future challenges.

PepsiCo's leadership-development strategy is grounded in the belief that strong leaders are needed to be successful in the marketplace. This belief is fundamental to PepsiCo's two-pronged HR approach, which includes a career-growth model and a talent-management model for leadership development. (See the PepsiCo case study in Part II.) This two-pronged HR approach aligns with corporate strategic initiatives, which in turn link with the organization's sustainable competitive advantage.

Cisco uses executive sponsors to tie its leadership-development strategy to its business strategy. To further strengthen this link, HR partnered with Global Operations to create the Global Leader Program in support of the company's worldwide strategy.

As we said, all best-practice partners closely tie their leadership-development strategies to their business strategies to ensure that emerging leaders are prepared to lead their respective organizations well into the future. Common sense would indicate that this tie is always present. Unfortunately it is not. Taking time to make this connection specific and deliberate is not common, but it is almost a requirement for excellence.

Communicating the Strategy

Key Finding 3. Executives use leadership development as a powerful tool to formulate, translate, and communicate strategy.

While education is a relatively small portion of the entire development process for leaders, carefully crafted learning initiatives are important for gathering input from people in the organization and communicating key themes to everyone in the firm. Learning programs can effectively communicate the reasons for and implications of corporate strategy to managers, who need to translate that strategy for employees so everyone understands his or her role in creating the desired future.

As previously mentioned, one of the components of Caterpillar's Leadership Quest program was having participants present to the CEO their strategy for the organization in the year 2020. In October 2005, the Strategic Planning Committee announced the organization's Vision 2020 and reformulated Code of Conduct. Immediately, the College of Leadership, in partnership with key enterprise organizations, rolled out the new strategy and code down through the organization using a leaders-as-teachers approach. Also in October, learning sessions designed to achieve divisional alignment were conducted around the world. Sessions designed to communicate the vision to employees were completed by the following January. Essentially, all leaders were involved in communicating the essence of the new strategy to their subordinates and helping them see their roles in achieving the organization's strategic goals.

In its discussion of how to create a positive organizational culture, PwC focused on its core values of leadership, excellence, and teamwork, along with the critical attributes of good client service, trust and quality. The PwC University Experience has proved to be an effective and efficient means of sharing information about the organization's direction with all of the firm's partners and moving its culture in the desired direction.

Various studies have concluded that 60 to 70 percent of all strategies fail to be successfully implemented. The best-practice partners beat these odds by ensuring that everyone in their organizations understood the strategy, the reasons for it, and their roles in implementation. These companies also understand that leadership-development activities can be an effective means of sharing information and providing tools for successful implementation of strategy. Leadership development is a bully pulpit for corporate leaders—a way for them to share their views of an organization's future and to engage future leaders in dialogues about strategy and challenges of implementation. Senior executives recognize that these conversations about strategy can challenge their own sometimes insular thinking, can leverage communication efforts by engaging several high-potential middle-level managers simultaneously, and can provide opportunities to clarify thinking and articulate key concepts. Moreover, the executives gain insights into the essential skills and capabilities of younger leaders from throughout the firm.

Lean Competency Models

> **Key Finding 4.** Lean competency models and values are the foundation of strategic leadership development.

Clearly, alignment is a key concept for successful implementation of leadership-development strategies. A simple leadership model with a concise statement of values can be the central focus for that alignment. None of the best-practice partners had a scientifically valid competency model; most had created their own strategy or had adapted a set of competencies developed by an outside organization. We found, however, that all of the partners and most (81 percent) of the sponsors identified and implemented lean leadership competencies within their organizations.

Almost all of the study participants recognized the need to identify and develop competencies that would ensure the success of their organizations into the future. In other words, most firms sense the necessity of understanding the competencies required for success and that this is the starting point for planning leadership development. However, organizations differ in the ways they use their competencies to connect the strategic needs of the organization to the challenges of developing their people. The organizations that were able to keep their competencies relatively simple, or lean, were more effective in applying those competencies than were those with more complex models.

In 2001, PepsiCo revised its leadership model based on new leadership and changes in strategic direction at the time to identify three leadership imperatives, seven success factors, and seventeen competency dimensions, as shown in Figure 2.5. Although all seventeen competencies are important, the three leadership imperatives focus employees on what is truly important. Interestingly, the three major clusters of Caterpillar's leadership competencies framework are very similar: vision (setting the agenda), execution (doing it the right way), and legacy (taking others with you).

Additionally, this study found that all of the best-practice partners and almost all (84 percent) of the sponsors indicated that the competency models have behaviors tied to them. Also, all of the best-practice partners have had competency models in place for approximately the same time as they have had leadership-development strategies in place.

A competency model can serve as a foundation for planning and

Figure 2.5. PepsiCo's leadership competency model.

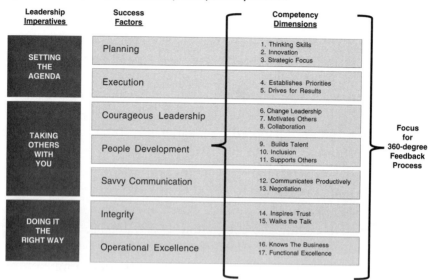

implementing a successful leadership-development strategy, especially if the models are developed in the context of a firm's future strategic direction. Washington Group relies on twelve competencies (referred to as "business skills" it believes to be critical to effective personal performance and thus to business performance. A business-skills booklet refers to them as the "softer skills" in contrast to technical or job-specific skills.

The connection between PwC's values and leadership framework is shown in Figure 2.6. This framework is tied to the organization's competencies and is often a foundation for leadership-development initiatives. Cisco uses its Grow Model ("Grow the business; Grow the team; Grow yourself") as its competency model. Each component of the model is tied to Cisco's cultural values (customers, teamwork, collaboration, integrity, judgment, and perspective).

The best-practice partners keep their values and competencies simple and straightforward. They understand that competencies should apply at all levels of an organization and directly lead to better performance. As we have shown, an integrated strategic leadership framework can add value to a business. Figure 2.7 can be helpful in addressing some of the key talent-management problems facing

Figure 2.6. PricewaterhouseCoopers' stated business values.

Our Values

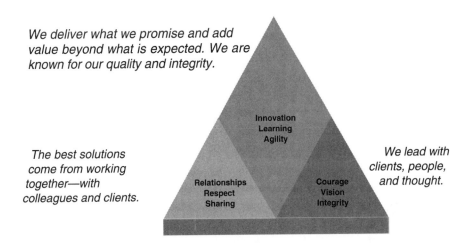

We deliver what we promise and add value beyond what is expected. We are known for our quality and integrity.

The best solutions come from working together—with colleagues and clients.

Innovation
Learning
Agility

Relationships
Respect
Sharing

Courage
Vision
Integrity

We lead with clients, people, and thought.

Figure 2.7. Context for setting leadership strategy.

Talent-Management Issues

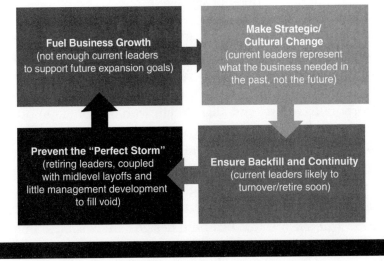

Fuel Business Growth
(not enough current leaders to support future expansion goals)

Make Strategic/ Cultural Change
(current leaders represent what the business needed in the past, not the future)

Prevent the "Perfect Storm"
(retiring leaders, coupled with midlevel layoffs and little management development to fill void)

Ensure Backfill and Continuity
(current leaders likely to turnover/retire soon)

SOURCE: Duke Corporate Education, 2007.

organizations today. Building content around these areas can help an organization ensure leadership continuity and prepare for future growth.

Leadership Strategy Development: Summary

Developing a leadership strategy requires organizational commitment, buy-in, and focus. Furthermore, creating and/or understanding an organization's culture and values are paramount before any leadership-development strategy can be designed and implemented. The essential elements for developing a successful leadership-development strategy are:

▲ Experiencing a teachable moment and coupling it with the opportunity to change the culture

▲ Establishing a corporate business strategy that is visionary, then linking the leadership-development strategy to it

▲ Engaging in conversations about the leadership vision and gaining support through the communication efforts

▲ Creating a lean competency model and the values that can guide the leadership-development strategy

A sound leadership-development strategy builds a foundation and infrastructure that cascade knowledge, understanding, and motivation down through the organization. Additionally, it provides opportunities to available talent, facilitates the assimilation of external hires into the corporate culture, and aligns them with the direction of the company. A leadership-development strategy affords employees an opportunity to grow and eventually excel.

Chapter 3 will reveal how developing a strategy is only a beginning. Design is the starting point; a successful leadership-development architecture requires commitment, application, integration, and synergy. Any architect will tell you that beautiful designs are worthless unless someone is committed to making the project become a reality. This will only happen when the owner is willing to commit time, money, and effort to making the design become a reality.

CHAPTER 3

Building an Aligned Architecture for Strategic Leadership Development

Chapter 2 discussed the importance of capitalizing on key moments, communicating an aligned strategy, and operating with lean competency models as a foundation for strategic leadership development. To build on that foundation, organizations must have a vision for the design and delivery of the strategy—a structure that shows how the related programs, activities, and systems work together to ensure success. For example, think about preparing to build a house. The property owners discuss the elements they want the house to include, usually expressed in terms of cost, function, and appearance. Because a house contains a variety of systems, each one must be considered in relation to the others. For instance, deciding to have twelve-foot ceilings will increase the cost and impact the design of heating and lighting systems. An architect listens to the owners' wishes, concerns, and limitations, then turns these ideas into a detailed plan.

A contractor or general foreman does not start building an entire house by randomly selecting a room. Instead, he or she reviews blueprints with floor plans and specifications so as to understand what type of dwelling it should be (single- or multi-family), the purpose of each room, how it will connect with others, and the infrastructure (e.g., wiring and plumbing) required. Construction starts with laying the foundation and moves on to framing the structure, installing the roof, and closing the outside walls before the plumbing and electricity are installed. The blueprint, or architectural design, shows the contractor how these different components fit together, provides required specifications, and gives references to be consulted regarding different components of the job. This blueprint aligns everyone associated with the project with what the owners expect to see when the project is completed.

The same could be said for organizations with true strategic leadership-development initiatives, such as the best-practice partners in this study. These organizations have an integrated architecture for their strategic leadership-development initiatives that helps the office or group responsible for implementing the strategy (usually HRD or employee development) understand how the programs align or build on one another and who the key stakeholders are—who will set direction, design and develop the programs, and deliver them.

Why is an integrated architecture important? As this (and Chapters 4 through 7) will demonstrate, architecture ensures that all components are aligned with common goals. Moreover, the architectural structure helps everyone in the organization understand how the leadership-development programs build on one another and contribute to the achievement of strategic goals. A well-designed architecture for leadership development can:

▲ Name which key stakeholders (e.g., executives, business units, and individuals) need to be involved in the direction, design, and delivery of the strategy and programs

▲ Provide leverage from these programs in support of the business strategy and the development of organizational capabilities in a strategic fashion

▲ Determine where and how to best identify and develop collective and individual capabilities

Bridging the Gap: Moving the Architecture from Vision to Reality

Our colleagues at Duke Corporate Education (Duke CE) use the template shown in Figure 3.1 to help clients see the connections between corporate strategies and business objectives, along with the leadership challenges and chances for development. The process starts with a clear understanding and articulation of the competitive environment as well as the strategic imperatives that grow out of this competitive analysis. This conversation typically involves senior line executives and strategically astute HRD professionals. The task of explaining the business challenges is often instructive for corporate representatives as well as for outside consultants. If these key corporate players have difficulty articulating the business challenges, that may be a harbinger of the firm's difficulty in implementing its strategy. Other leaders in the firm may not adequately understand the strategic imperatives or be fully supportive. Duke CE tries to tie all educational interventions to key business issues. In this way, educational efforts are more likely to have an impact and be viewed as successful.

After there's an understanding of the business issues involved, the next task is to review the challenges associated with current and projected leadership capabilities. In other words, will new competencies be required for leaders to reach the goals set for the organization? What managerial levels will benefit most from or have the most impact in addressing these challenges? Does the culture of the organization need to change in order for the company to be strategically successful?

Finally, the program-development group (the architects) looks at previous design concepts to determine what will be most helpful to the organization (client) in achieving its vision. The resulting plan is a blueprint for business success, as illustrated in Figure 3.1. Duke CE's unique approach to advising clients about the architecture for

Figure 3.1. Duke CE's template for strategic architecture.

Competitive Environment	Strategic Imperatives	Business Challenges	Leadership Capabilities	Leadership Development
• What's big and new? Which pressures are you facing? • External forces for change – Environment – Competition – Industry evolution – Demographics – Regulation • Internal forces for change – Current change initiatives – Employee satisfaction levels – Turnover – Recruitment difficulties – Outsourcing – Off-shoring	• What is the scale and scope of change that you are facing? • Business Consistency: – E.g.: challenges of cost containment, quality, efficiency • Business Evolution: • E.g., challenges of divergence/convergence, new and unexpected competition, adjustments in the value chain • Business Revolution: • E.g. challenges of discontinuity, evolution of entirely new business model, long-term players' sudden demise	• Which key challenges are you facing? Which organizational capabilities do you need to build? • Examples: – Global expansion – Mind-set change from cost cutting to creating value – From passive to active selling – Collaboration for cross-sell, up-sell – Shared services integration for efficiency – Sustaining rapid growth – Innovation to stay ahead	• Which capabilities do you need to develop? Which offer the highest leverage for business impact? • New Competencies • Key Managerial Levels • Transitions – Promotions – Moving to new geographies/cross-cultural – Same function but different business – Same place, same business but different work	• Which interventions make most sense for developing your people? What is the map? • Examples include: – On-boarding – Job rotations – Secondments – Mentoring – Business-advisory coaching – Leadership coaching – Assessment – Action learning – Consortia – External board participation – CEO conferences – Leaders teaching leaders

(Top of figure: Vision | Business Challenges | Strategy Execution)

strategic leadership development is based on the seven principles we listed in Chapter 2.

The remainder of this chapter focuses on several aspects of the Duke CE template, such as the partnership between executives and HR, integration with the corporate planning calendar, using executives in strategic learning initiatives as contributors or teachers, and a focus on high potentials.

Partnerships Between Senior Executives and Human Resources Personnel

Key Finding 5. Strategic leadership development involves a conscious partnership between senior executives and multiple human resource systems.

Senior-executive support, usually starting with the CEO, is vital for the success of any strategic leadership development. The best and most ambitious human resources team cannot create this partnership and achieve alignment without support from line management. Similarly, even the most effective CEO cannot ensure success without involving an organization's entire human resource system (e.g., training and development, assessment, talent management/succession planning systems, performance-management systems, etc.).

Executives in key staff positions may be tempted to develop their reputations in their professional specialties rather than achieve prominence within the firm that employs them—after all, the next job offer is likely to be based on contacts outside the firm. However, the best professional reputations are built on people's being strategic partners and contributors to their organizations' success rather than on their speeches at professional meetings. Human resource professionals in general, and HRD leaders in particular, will not be successful in their careers unless they collaborate with their colleagues in line positions. These partnerships are not likely to just happen. They must be built on a shared recognition that, by working together to achieve business goals, individuals can be more successful than if they work alone.

All of the study's partners indicated that senior management at their organizations place a high to very high priority on leadership development. This compares with about two-thirds of the sponsor organizations (see Figure 3.2). Nevertheless, both best-practice partners and sponsors agreed that leadership development is an area of increasing importance for strategic success. These organizations recognize the importance of developing leaders to carry the organization into the future and they agree that this skill set should be part of that development. Indeed, the broad support and collaborative engagement are vital to setting the organization's agenda and leaving a legacy.

Lombardo and Eichinger have suggested that leadership development is a composite of activities that includes three major components: on-the-job experience, feedback and role models, and formal educational programs.[1] The most important capacity building happens when people are required to do challenging work that adds value to an organization and are given helpful feedback about their performance. Their research emphasizes the overwhelming value of work in the developmental process, estimating that about 70 percent

Figure 3.2. How high a priority does your organization's senior management give to leadership development?

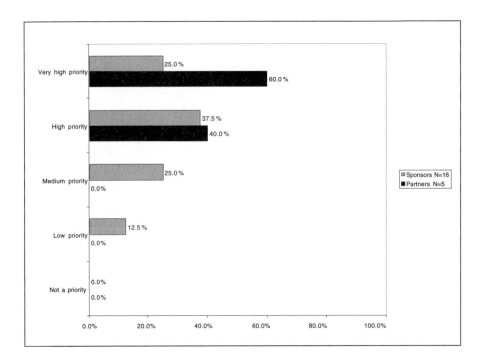

of personal growth comes from learning on the job—working on real tasks and problems. Their model resonates with professionals in the field, who believe that about 20 percent of employee development stems from coaching, acting on feedback, or mimicking role models. These professionals also believe that approximately 10 percent of development stems from learning through courses, educational initiatives, or reading.

In order to coordinate their development activities, our best-practice partners have developed programs that integrate all aspects of the human resource systems. While accepting the idea that learning programs may constitute only 10 percent of the total development package, they seem to believe that, executed effectively, educational programs could be a major leveraging agent to improve the effectiveness of other developmental initiatives.

An illustration of the linkage between human resource systems, Caterpillar's leadership framework joins other core processes, such as selection, development, performance management, succession management, and career management, as shown in Figure 3.3. Global experience, as well as cross-functional assignments and involvement in the company's emphasis on Six Sigma and other work experience, make up 70 percent of leadership development. Performance management, individual development plans, multirater feedback, coaching and mentoring or serving as role models, and the "Leaders as Teachers" program constitute approximately 20 percent of the development process. Finally, continuing education and continual learning make up a vital 10 percent of this coordinated system.

Caterpillar University's College of Leadership is responsible for the design of Caterpillar's leadership-development programs. However, the college's senior learning consultants receive valuable input for program design from senior executives as well as the lead learning

Figure 3.3. The Caterpillar Leadership Framework—integration into core HR processes.

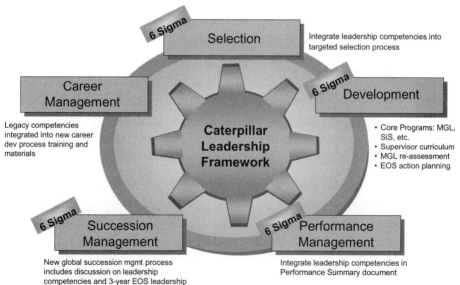

managers in the organization's thirty business units. This helps ensure alignment between the programs' objectives and the business.

The PepsiCo model (see Figure 3.4) shows these components as part of the annual operating plan, thus graphically depicting the link between the corporate planning calendar and strategic leadership development.

Within Cisco's HR function, the organization's Worldwide Leadership Development group works with the business's leaders to identify candidates for its key educational programs. Senior executives nominate these candidates through the leadership review process. Additionally, business partners, or executive sponsors, work with Worldwide Leadership Development program managers and program coordinator teams to design the programs in the leadership series. Each program has an executive sponsor and steering committee that ensure the program meets business needs and aligns with strategy.

The process of developing PricewaterhouseCoopers LLP's leadership strategy is inclusive and involves representatives from each of PwC's lines of service (assurance, tax, and advisory services), Learn-

Figure 3.4. Connecting PepsiCo people processes.

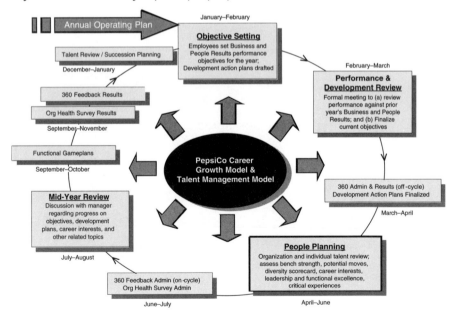

ing & Education, HR, the U.S. Leadership Team, and Partner Affairs. For example, the Learning & Education team works with vendors such as Duke CE along with the U.S. firm's management committee to develop and deploy the PwC University program. Additionally, the firm's leaders work with the Learning & Education team to deliver PwC's SOAR program (described in detail in the PwC case study). Finally, in the PwC University 2 experience, the Learning & Education team works with local-area partners and managers to ensure their business-area needs were met.

At Washington Group, corporate and the business units share responsibility for leadership development. The integrated Strategic Staffing and Talent Management group is responsible for the design, development, implementation, and maintenance of the programs, and the office of the chairman reviews, approves, and provides feedback on moving forward with developmental proposals. The fourteen-member senior-executive leadership team meets regularly to discuss leadership development.

One way to ensure that something gets done in an organization is to embed the process or job in the workflow. As the next section will show, this has been accomplished with strategic leadership development at the partner organizations by linking people-development processes to the corporate calendar.

Embedding Strategic Leadership Development

Key Finding 6. Strategic HRD is a key part of the corporate planning cycle.

If developing leaders is a strategic priority for a company, the odds are that there is an HRD component to the business planning cycle. The American Productivity and Quality Center (APQC)'s 2005 study, titled "Next Generation Human Resources: Driving Organizational Excellence," found that a strong relationship between HRD and the corporate calendar is crucial if HR is to be a true partner in the organization's strategic process. In that study, it was found that the best-practice partners developed that partnership in two ways: (1) by formulating strategies that contribute to the organization's strategic goals during the same time as business units developed their objectives, and (2) by conducting leadership reviews during the same time as conducting business and operational reviews. In this most recent study's survey, all best-practice partners indicated that leadership development is tied to the corporate planning calendar, as compared to only 37.5 percent of the study's sponsors.

As with the best-practice organizations in the 2005 research, this study's best-practice partners tend to make people planning, as well as succession management, a matter all key executives are expected to address in concert with their human resource partners and the immediate supervisors of the people being evaluated. In other words, identifying the key players expected to implement corporate strategy, and considering the assistance they may need to enhance the probability of success, is a natural part of the corporate planning cycle.

Washington Group leverages its annual strategic and business planning sessions to discuss employee development and leadership-development needs for the organization. Information on economic issues, industry trends, and the group's own organizational performance is used to evaluate the leadership-development process and to make recommendations for changes to the strategy.

PepsiCo's People Processes align exactly with the organization's annual operating calendar. Figure 3.4 shows that each stage of the planning cycle includes a specific focus on key people issues. Leaders at PepsiCo would be hard-pressed to miss the message that leadership strategy is integral to the overall corporate strategy.

Caterpillar's College of Leadership conducts its learning-needs assessments with the organization's thirty business units as part of the annual corporate planning cycle. This allows for both a short-term view (needs for the next year) and a more long-term view.

Key Findings 5 and 6 lead to a strong conclusion that the successful development of leaders requires a strategic alignment of planning and all human resource systems. Let's now consider the role of top management in leadership development.

Winning Top-Management Support

Key Finding 7. HRD can win the support of top management by involving it in strategic learning initiatives and by understanding the business.

Most of the exemplars in this study have a high degree of executive involvement in the delivery of key corporate programs. Executive involvement in program design can ensure that the program content addresses topics of genuine concern to key constituencies and can contribute to higher levels of support for the ongoing initiative.

For most of the study's participants, responsibility for the organization's leadership-development strategy is shared between corporate and the business units (see Figure 3.5). This collaboration is important because, if done correctly, it ensures that the challenges faced by the business units are being addressed appropriately through the leadership-development programs. In other words, alignment of leadership-development strategy and business strategy requires a partnership among corporate HRD, divisional HR managers, and line managers.

The different individuals or functions responsible for designing and implementing leadership-development strategy include the board of directors, the CEO, the COO/CFO/CIO, divisional executives, human resources, learning and development, and individual business units (among others). Study participants were asked what role these functions or individuals play with regard to leadership development. As Figure 3.6 shows, the best-practice partners really engage their executives in the direction and delivery of leadership-development strategy. The HR and learning-and-development groups work with the executives to understand the business strategy, which often determines the direction of the leadership-development strategy. They also work to engage them in the delivery.

Our exemplars believe that external faculty and subject-matter experts don't always tailor their programs so that the content has mean-

Figure 3.5. Does responsibility for your leadership-development strategy reside at the corporate or business-unit level?

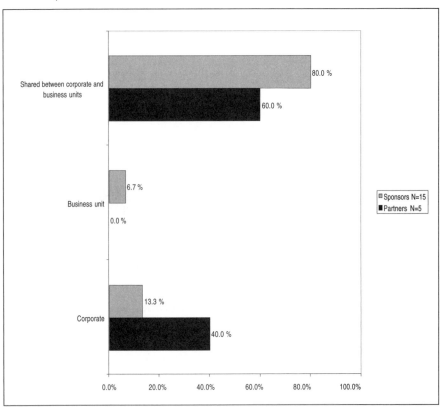

ing for the participants. Also, program participants often learn best from people they know, admire, and respect. Figure 3.6 suggests that best-practice firms are much more likely to have top management involved in the governance and delivery of leadership development than are the comparison firms.

When asked to approximate the percentage of the CEO's time spent on issues associated with leadership development, three of the five study partners indicated that their CEOs spend anywhere from 11 to 50 percent of their time on such issues. This is a huge commitment and shows just how strongly these organizations feel about leadership development. These results mirror a 2005 study of top firms for lead-

Figure 3.6. Percentage of key executives involved in leadership development.

Organizational Entity	Direction		Design		Delivery		Measurement	
	Partner	Sponsor	Partner	Sponsor	Partner	Sponsor	Partner	Sponsor
Board of Directors	60	44	0	0	0	0	0	19
CEO	100	69	20	25	60	19	20	25
COO/CFO/CIO	100	25	0	19	60	19	0	25
Divisional Executives	100	57	0	19	80	44	0	25
Human Resources	100	75	40	69	80	81	40	56
Learning and Development	100	50	100	63	100	75	100	44
Individual Business Units	80	31	60	38	60	63	60	38

ers (Salob and Greenslade), in which all of the top twenty companies cited reported strong CEO involvement and sponsorship for leadership development. This is compared to 65 percent of the comparison firms.

Our study also confirms the findings of a 2004 survey of the executive education practices in twenty-eight global organizations (Saslow). This study found that "aligning development and corporate goals" was a key priority of the best-performing companies. Firms that had previously practiced a bottom-up approach, which starts with individuals and the skills they need, shifted their emphasis to building programs around corporate goals and current initiatives.

At Cisco, each program has an established cross-functional executive-steering committee that tightens the link between the program and the business. The business leaders on the steering committees help drive the design of the programs and recruit appropriate executives for the classrooms. In addition, they play the roles of coach and facilitator and host networking events in the program. The programs typically employ executive faculty, or internal leaders who bring participants a strategic perspective.

A board of governors for Caterpillar University, which includes the CEO and senior executives, approves learning budgets and priorities and also determines policy. An advisory board for each college includes senior leaders from business or user groups. This group is diverse in terms of geography and subject-matter expertise and has members from most of Caterpillar's business units.

Before each leadership-development program is rolled out, PwC's design team consults with a committee of designated leader-partners who serve as a strategic sounding board to ensure alignment. The U.S. business's management committee, the organization's highest leadership team, is highly involved in all decisions regarding partner leadership development. Members of this committee attend key partner programs where they speak or lead and engage in discussions. They may also participate in the program alongside other partners and participants.

A meeting between Washington Group's HR team and the office of the chairman led to the development of the organization's LEAP (Leadership Excellence and Performance) program. (For more details on this program, see the case study in Part II.) Members of the senior leadership team also serve as instructors in Washington Group's Leaders Forum. Key officers design and deliver the material for the forum. For example, the CFO designed a method to help participants better understand financial matters using an electronic board game patterned after the popular television program *Jeopardy!*

Although it is important to involve line executives who have a deep understanding of the business challenges facing an organization in key leadership-development decisions, this involvement is not sufficient to ensure program success. HRD partners must understand the business as well as cutting-edge leadership concepts in order to focus executive interests on ways of leadership development that incorporate internal challenges and external best practices. In this study, the partners' HRD staffs are keenly aware of what is happening outside the enterprise, especially in the arena of leadership development. Most use outside specialists to supplement their understanding of the latest thinking in the external world. All of the best-practice partners emphasized the importance of understanding both the business and the strategy of their companies.

Engaging Effective Leaders

Key Finding 8. Leaders who teach are more effective than those who tell.

One of the surprising findings of this project is the degree to which senior executives practice the concept of leading by teaching. At PepsiCo, Paul Russell, vice president of executive learning & development, spoke of "the magic of leaders developing leaders." Using leaders to teach other leaders is a large part of PepsiCo's approach to leadership development.

In a recent high-potential program, nineteen of Caterpillar's thirty-six officers (including all members of the executive office) participated in the semiannual Leadership Quest. As noted, Caterpillar has a strong commitment to supporting the leaders-as-teachers concept and used this philosophy to involve almost all of its mangers in the late 2005 rollout of the new corporate strategy and code of conduct. The Leadership College of Caterpillar University has prepared a twelve-page document titled "Leaders as Teachers." It speaks proudly of involving more than 600 leaders in the rollout of its new code of conduct and enterprise strategy, "Vision 2020," in late 2005. More than 84,000 employees were reached by this initiative.

When we discussed this finding during a knowledge transfer session, when we reviewed our findings with the study sponsors, one of them commented, "The last thing I want is to have my officers in front of a group of high potentials. They are such terrible presenters, it would ruin the program." One of the best-practice partners responded, "In our organization, a person doesn't become an officer unless he or she is an effective communicator."

Some of the partners leverage their leaders as coaches and/or mentors as part of their organization's leadership-development activities (see Figure 3.7). This is crucial as it helps build relationships across generations of leaders, gives current leaders deeper insight into the next generation, enables the transfer of tacit knowledge (through sharing critical experiences, war stories, and lessons learned)

Figure 3.7. Are current leaders used as coaches and/or mentors in the leadership-development programs?

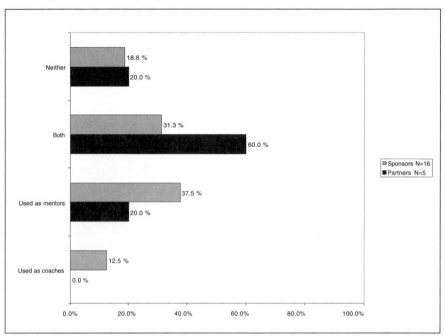

from one cohort to the next, and helps create a legacy—described as a core leadership competency in Chapter 2.

For example, participants in Washington Group's LEAP program are assigned a mentor for one year. This mentor is a member of the executive team, and he or she is expected to work with the protégé to develop an action plan. Additionally, LEAP participants have the opportunity to meet and interact with the company's board members. The relationships developed between the high potentials and the leaders involved in LEAP become teaching experiences for the participants, who in turn become leaders and mentors for their subordinates.

Additionally, the company's senior leadership is not only actively involved in the nomination and selection process for key leadership courses, but they also serve as instructors. The office of the chairman and retired executives share their experiences in the project-management arena, which serves to transfer knowledge and mentor this up-and-coming group of leaders.

Knowledge Transfer Across Generations of Leaders

A growing concern across many HRD functions is the bench strength of the leadership pipeline at their organizations. This study's participants are no different. Many factors impact that bench strength, including baby boomer retirement, an increasingly mobile workforce, and a decreasing number of people entering organizations with the needed skills and capabilities. Study participants expressed interest in what the best-practice partners are currently doing to prevent the loss of critical organizational and business knowledge and to transfer this knowledge to the next generation in order to keep it in-house, prevent reinvention of basic concepts, reduce mistakes, and avoid the loss of hard-won organizational capabilities.

To combat that potential loss, many of the study's partners engage executives in leadership-development opportunities as a way to transfer knowledge to the next generation of leaders in the organization. Here are some of the approaches and/or tools the partners use for this purpose:

▲ *Use leaders as teachers.* This is a way to share experiences and insights and thus increase the bench strength of the next generation of leaders and allow for continual knowledge transfer.

▲ *Use cross-generational participants.* This populates the leadership-development activities with participants of various ages in order to encourage knowledge transfer in an informal manner.

▲ *Leverage job assignments/rotations.* Exposure to new challenges, perspectives, leaders and leadership styles, situations, learnings, and real-life experiences increases knowledge transfer.

▲ *Use mentoring and coaching.* Relevant, business-based coaching relationships help transfer knowledge and insights.

▲ *Make use of facilitated small-group discussion.* Senior partners transfer knowledge through storytelling, dialogue, and discussion with more junior partners.

An Integrated Architecture for Leadership Development: Summary

One of the most popular ways to transfer knowledge among best-practice partners is to engage leaders as teachers where they share experiences, war stories, lessons learned, and personal challenges with the emerging or future leaders. Many competency models include a category called "Leaving a Legacy." Leaders who teach by word and by action are making a significant contribution to their legacies when they share their vision and insights with the next generation. Developing the cadre of people with the highest potential offers a high return for both the organization and the individuals involved. Ultimately, crafting a leadership-development strategy lays the groundwork for a successful high-potential program, which can in turn lead to successful implementation of a leadership-development strategy. We explore this challenge in Chapter 4.

Implementing Successful Strategic Leadership Development

In Chapter 3, we established the specific benefits that an organization can reap from the deliberate and structured development of high-potential leaders. We've seen how the process of strategizing this development is both methodical and meticulous—and unique to each organization studied. But how does an organization establish a consistent, systematic method to prepare candidates for key positions? How should the appropriate programs and applications be implemented? Indeed, how should this vital blueprint be drafted? In this chapter, we listen in on the five conversations that are needed to build and implement a leadership-development strategy. We see what the best-practice companies in our study have in common when it comes to leadership development. And finally, we explore two useful modalities for jump-starting, and then inculcating, leadership development in an organization.

Making It Happen: Moving from Objectives to Implementation

Because a forward-looking organization aims to groom its future leaders, an ability to sense its future needs, in both its leadership-development strategy and project plans, is essential for success. Successful implementation, then, is predicated on the relevance and real-time nature of the programs and applications it develops.

Several factors come into play. An intimate knowledge of an organization's needs, culture, values, goals, and overall vision is required, as is integration of the entire talent-management system. Accordingly, programs developed internally tend to have applicability, relevance, and longevity. Also, when talent-management systems—such as leadership development, succession planning, performance management, and management development—work synergistically, a leadership-development strategy is more likely to yield success.

In our work with global clients, we've identified half a dozen critical objectives for building and implementing a strategic leadership-development framework. You'll recognize the first three from Chapters 1 through 3.

1. Understanding and articulating an integrated leadership strategy for the company.

2. Drafting a roadmap for new leadership.

3. Developing a leader practices/competencies model and needs-assessment survey.

4. Creating a leader talent-management process, wherein the components of a talent-management system support each other as well as the overall corporate strategy. (Figure 4.1 illustrates how one company accomplished this.)

5. Building an implementation plan for the development of key programs and interventions. (Creating a plan is an excellent start, but proceeding without a strategy for implementation is short-sighted—and a recipe for failure.)

6. Supporting the rollout of high-leverage initiatives for the future. (We have discussed the importance of winning support from sen-

Figure 4.1. Aligning the talent-management process for building a leadership pipeline.

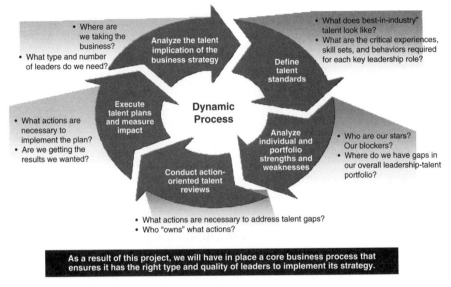

ior management in Chapter 3; its involvement and support is essential for inaugurating new initiatives.)

This chapter—indeed, this entire book—emphasizes the importance of partnerships between HRD and line executives, as well as between lean HRD staffs and their outside advisers or providers. Using the insights gained from studying top-performing companies worldwide, Duke CE has developed the five-part list of objectives that are the topic of this chapter. These objectives will help you:

▲ Analyze how well your organization's leadership strategy meets the challenge of its business strategy

▲ Apply a proven approach, using proven tools, to build your leadership strategy, architecture, and pipeline

▲ Assess your leadership portfolio and identify high-leverage initiatives

▲ Design and deliver the world-class programs and business-action learning that drive strategy execution

▲ Align and engage your organization for successful implementation of these programs

Critical Conversations for Successful Development and Implementation of Leadership Programs

Each year from 2002 to 2007, the *Financial Times* named Duke Corporate Education (Duke CE) the number-one source in the world for custom-designed executive-education programs. We believe that this recognition has come to Duke CE because it has developed a process for engaging its clients in critical conversations about their businesses and leadership strategies. Duke's five key topics are shown in Figure 4.2. Based on these conversations, Duke CE has developed a series of templates that help clients identify critical issues. Most of these critical questions are straightforward and intended to initiate discussion of key issues.

1. *Determine destination.* The first topic deals with the organization's vision or destination. The major objective is to create a shared

Figure 4.2. Five conversations to build and implement your leadership strategy.

Conversation 1 Determine Destination	Conversation 2 Define Guiding Principles and Current Reality	Conversation 3 Create the New Leadership Roadmap	Conversation 4 Review and Align the Infrastructure	Conversation 5 Measure
• What is our shared vision? • What leadership skills are important in our organization? • What is the competitive environment? • What are the business challenges? • How will we know when we achieve our vision? (What are the results, e.g., talent, organization, financial?)	• What is the leadership philosophy/principles? • What are the organization capabilities required to drive future business success? • What specific leadership practices and behaviors are required? (eg., competencies or leadership framework) • What is the existing portfolio of development planning and key experiences? • What is the state of the leadership pipeline?	• What is the existing portfolio of development programs and experiences (eg., current reality)? • What is the new leadership roadmap? • What is the development curriculum by level and role? • What do the development solutions look like for on-job and off-job opportunities? • What aspects of the roadmap are urgent priority, midterm, and low priorities?	• What processes, supports, routines, and technology are needed to support the new leadership strategy and architecture? • What capabilities are required? • What is the implementation plan? • What is the communication plan?	• What does success look like? • What will the audience know/do/believe differently? • How can you quantify and verify that you've reached your destination?
• Shared vision w/results • Map of strategic imperatives • Business challenges • Line leader validation	• Leadership principles and core messages • Leadership capabilities • Leader pipeline gap analysis • Line leader validation	• High-level roadmap • Identification of leadership pipeline • Prioritization of all initiatives • Leverage points • Line leader validation	• Infrastructure analysis • Implementation plan • Communication plan and key stakeholders • Line leader validation	• Gap analysis of leadership pipeline • Analysis of development curriculum • Line leader validation

SOURCE: Duke Corporate Education, 2007.

view of the desired future of the organization, along with some specific ways of recognizing success. In some instances, an overview of strategic imperatives is developed along with an articulation of supporting business challenges. Involving line leadership in this process to validate the assumptions created as a result of this conversation is also quite important.

2. *Define guiding principles and current reality.* The major thrust of the second conversation topic is to identify the values or principles that define the organization's culture. This conversation also includes an audit of current reality, so as to identify any gap between vision and reality. Closing this gap then becomes the target of subsequent activities.

3. *Create the new leadership blueprint.* The third conversation topic looks at the organization's existing portfolio of programs and its experiences and then compares that with the proposed leadership design. This step begins the process of creating a new curriculum, as well as adjusting existing aspects of the talent-management process. Figure 4.3 depicts a blueprint for developing this leadership strategy, with the gaps between vision and solutions that need to be bridged.

4. *Review and align the infrastructure.* The fourth conversation topic involves reviewing, adjusting, and aligning the infrastructure required to support the new leadership-development strategy. At this point, an implementation plan is created and responsibilities are assigned for achieving specific targets, as well as a process is started for communicating the new realities to all involved, whether program sponsors or participants.

5. *Measure.* The final topic focuses conversation on determining how success will be measured, what specific results are expected, and which behaviors should be changed. This topic is discussed in significantly greater detail in Chapter 6.

Three Keys to Architectural Success

In this chapter, we focus on several aspects of implementing a successful leadership-development strategy. The success of most steps in

Figure 4.3. A blueprint for strategic leadership development.

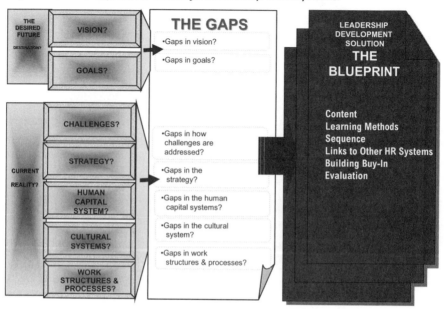

SOURCE: Duke Corporate Education, 2007.

the process will depend on an optimum mixture of internal and external development, as well as full integration of the talent-management
system.

Continuing our presentation of our study's key findings, we find
three more principal similarities among the best-practice companies,
in this case regarding development of a leadership strategy.

Leaders Are Actively Involved in the Process

Key Finding 9. HRD owns the process and maintains strategic control.

We were surprised to find the degree to which the exemplar firms
maintained control of the design and delivery of their leadership-
development programs. All had relatively small yet dedicated staffs
for the HRD function—and none had delegated significant control to
outsiders. They typically exercised influence over succession planning, training and development, and performance management, even

though they often shared implementation with various business units. This unique characteristic aligns with the development programs that are tailor-made to meet specific organizational needs and the strategic focus of their organizations.

Each best-practice partner has specific operational and strategic objectives; achieving these goals requires in-house control of the design and implementation of leadership-development programs.

Based on this research, best-practice partners design their leadership-development programs to address specific corporate challenges, with occasional adaptations to address unique business-unit challenges or organizational cultures. As Figure 4.4 shows, the partners in the study are significantly better at this than are the sponsors. Is this due to the maturity of their leadership-development strategies and programs? This is certainly possible.

Consider PricewaterhouseCoopers. As a professional services firm, PwC has greater involvement with outside professionals, believing that its partners' time can be better spent helping its own clients rather than trying to become experts in HRD. Although the firm's Learning & Education Group boasts some 240 employees, most of

Figure 4.4. Does the implementation of your leadership-development initiatives answer the following?

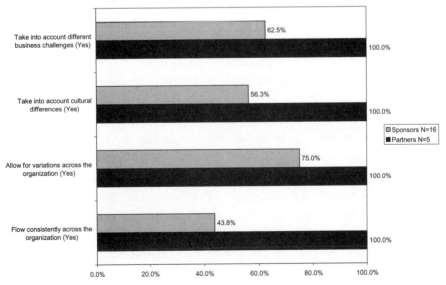

them are involved in technical and professional learning. Only a very small subset is dedicated to leadership and partner development. However, these employees are totally involved in every aspect of the group's programs, even though the plan relies on external vendors for considerable design and delivery support. For the past several years, this group has worked with Duke CE, among other vendors, for support with most of its key leadership programs. In this arrangement, the firm's internal professionals are the link between the vendors and the firm's leadership, ensuring that plans, content, and delivery fit the expectations, needs, and standards of PwC partners.

While 100 percent of the best-practice partners use their learning and development departments to implement their leadership programs, 80 percent of the partners share this responsibility with a third party—three times as often as do our sponsors. In other words, the best partners believe that they can learn from outside specialists (see Figure 4.5). Some of the best-practice partners might like to "do it all," but this is simply not practical at a time when most organizations run lean. So these best-practice organizations prioritize their needs regarding development, design, and delivery in-house in order to meet specific organizational and program needs. However, given these companies' often-constrained resources, coupled with their recognition that they are not experts in all things, the best-practice partners use third-party providers when necessary and appropriate. In the end, though, final control and decisions about content and approach belong to the internal professionals, since they are responsible for results.

Washington Group's leadership development is heavily influenced by senior leadership and is coordinated by the senior vice president of human resources, a vice president of integrated staffing and talent management, and a director of employee development. This trio employs outside consultants only to a limited degree, relying instead on its own officers to do much of the actual instruction. Washington Group also makes use of former executives who have taken early retirement but still know the firm, its culture, and the industry.

Figure 4.5. Who is responsible for the implementation (and success) of leadership-development programs in your organization?

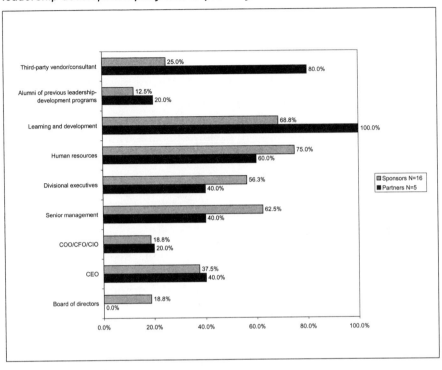

This part-time use of recent retirees ensures that their "consultants" understand the culture—and enjoy credibility among participants. The firm's leveraging of its own veterans also helps reduce the effects of the brain drain often associated with the departure of wise senior executives.

Finally, Caterpillar worked closely with the Hay Group to establish its Making Great Leaders program, which deploys the Caterpillar Leadership Framework. The company also turned to Duke CE for help in designing and facilitating its Leadership Quest program and in coaching its officers when they planned the course sessions. As we've seen, while leadership development remains firmly under the control of these best-practice partner corporations, their corporate staffs leverage their time and talents with the judicious use of outside experts.

Making Partners of Outside Providers

Key Finding 10. Lean human resources departments leverage their talents by partnering with outside experts.

The HRD leaders in the study maintained tight control of their programs while leveraging their time and skills via selective partnerships with outside specialists, as well as with other human resource colleagues within the company. As just mentioned, perhaps because of their emphasis on knowing the business and on lean staffing, most of the best-practice partners involve outside firms or specialists in both the design and delivery of their learning initiatives. They expect these outsiders to bring specialized talent to the table, plus learn and understand the client's business. However, no matter how busy they are, these professionals never entirely relinquish the tasks of program design and delivery.

PricewaterhouseCoopers probably delegates more of its education function to outside providers than do the other firms studied. As mentioned, the firm believes it is better served by letting its partners focus on their own professional expertise (which generates revenues for the firm) while hiring others to handle program design and delivery. Still, PwC's partners remain involved in every aspect of the process, using their internal access to ensure that activities address genuine business challenges. Washington Group, as we have seen, uses recently retired executives as an adjunct to its limited staff. Caterpillar, on the other hand, develops a few long-term relationships with outside consultants to provide an external perspective on its leaders-as-teachers approach.

The power of partnerships in the leadership-development process is important. We revisit that topic at the end of this chapter, along with providing some suggestions for making these partnerships successful.

Integration Amplifies Success

Key Finding 11. Integration of leadership development with other talent-management systems creates valuable synergies.

In none of the best-practice partners is leadership development an island or silo. There is a growing trend toward partnership with and alignment of succession planning and performance management, as well as other HR activities. Compared with the first APQC study of leadership development, our recent research revealed far more integration and alignment. Among the best-practice partners in this study, the leadership-development silo is little more than a crumbling relic of days past.[1]

Why is this so? For starters, organizations committed to leadership development understand its relationship to other talent-management systems and practices, and they seek to parlay that relationship into results. Thus, the best-practice partners incorporate their leadership-development programs with other programs such as performance institutes, management development, and succession planning. Interestingly, 60 percent of the best-practice partners have integrated their leadership-development programs with other talent-management systems. And the other 40 percent at least share common objectives across talent-management systems (see Figure 4.6). A significant portion of the sponsors (44%) have also taken steps to integrate their leadership-development programs with other talent-management systems to some degree. Let's look at how they have done this.

▲ *Human Capital.* The best-practice partners have invested heavily in their people. This, rather logically, predisposes them to integrate leadership development with other talent-management systems in order to receive the maximum possible benefit. Washington Group, for example, is such a strong proponent of this mindset that it aligns every aspect of talent management. The group's leadership-development strategy begins with its program 2020 Vision, which poses the provocative question: "Who will be instrumental in realizing the future?" It also attempts to anticipate what positions will need to be filled. Once this has been established, Washington Group begins forecasting, identifying, and preparing high-potential candidates for high-level executive and management positions (succession planning). After this phase is completed, employee-development plans are crafted for each candidate.

Figure 4.6. How closely is leadership development integrated with other talent-management systems such as succession planning and/or performance management?*

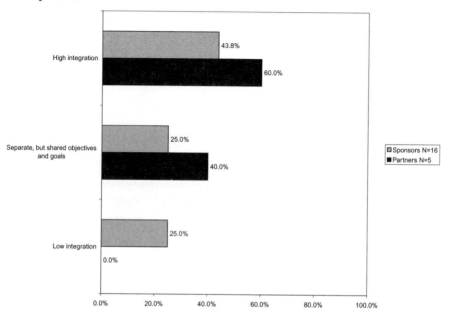

*Responses do not always add up to 100% as respondents were asked to "check all that apply."

This overall process is central to the development of leaders at Washington Group. Consequently, Washington Group uses its employee-development strategic plan to feed the succession-planning process, which in turn is used in its leadership-development program. The organization also uses its performance institute and management-development program to advance its leadership-development strategy.

How does Caterpillar integrate its efforts? Its succession-planning group works closely with the College of Leadership to provide high potentials with some of the experiences and opportunities they need to succeed. Thus, succession planning supports the nomination of individuals to attend the company's Leadership Quest program for high potentials. The succession-planning group ties its assessments and developmental planning to the same set of key competencies emphasized in Caterpillar's educational program and then helps establish the context of development for all future leaders.

At Caterpillar, succession planning works at all levels and in all business units. As we've shown in Chapter 2, selection, development, performance management, succession management, and career planning are all aligned with the Caterpillar leadership framework, which provides the core of the firm's leadership strategy.

▲ *Executive Coaches.* Figure 4.7 shows that 60 percent of the best-practice partners aligned and integrated executive coaching with other leadership-development activities. About half of the sponsors keep the activities separate but maintain congruent objectives for all leadership-development activities. This alignment is important because it helps ensure that participants receive the additional developmental support they need—and that this support meshes with the program's overarching objectives.

Cisco uses executive coaches to accelerate the development of its high potentials in its leadership-development programs. Each of these

Figure 4.7. How closely are executive coaching activities and other leadership-development programs aligned with each other?

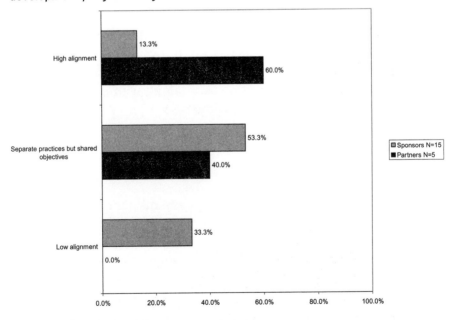

"high-po" candidates is paired for a year with an external executive coach. And even though the coach is an external resource, he or she is fully trained and well-versed in the Cisco way.

PricewaterhouseCoopers also uses executive coaches to enhance its leadership-development programs. Coaching activities are fundamental to PwC—so much so that coaching is a key competency in the firm's competency model. Employees at PwC are encouraged to coach others by participating in the performance-feedback process.

One particular area of focus should be the action plans for implementing the organization's key strategies. Action-learning projects can be specifically geared to leading the organization into the future. Development of strategic thinking and planning skills, or of basic business acumen, will stimulate the firm's leadership to act on the need for learning linked to the organization's future. Program initiatives should develop common frameworks, language, and understanding of strategic planning—and of the organization's business strategy.

Another area of focus should be on understanding the behaviors (often formalized as competencies) that lead to achievement of the organization's business strategies. These competencies are captured in the leadership capabilities that permeate all programs; they subsequently form the basis for individual development, linked to the assessment and evaluation efforts already under way. Consistent use of competencies, or a leadership framework, as a foundation for the assessment of potential or performance (along with educational initiatives) is a critical step in achieving the organization's strategic goals and meeting its talent needs.

Strategic Partnerships for Leadership Development

The finding that best-practice HR departments judiciously employ outside consultants in their pursuit of leadership development invites further discussion, as hinted at earlier in this chapter. Indeed, one of the overarching themes that emerged from our research is the vital nature of collaborations or partnerships with all parties involved in the development of future leaders. Each program, intervention, and interaction should have a clear business purpose that focuses on the future. Each should clearly lead to actions that align with the company's overall strategy.

What role should outsiders play in this multilayered drama? Quite simply, outside providers become their clients' business partners. As partners, both parties have a stake in the successful development of the organization's leaders over time. But forming a business partnership is easier said than done. Forging balanced partnerships requires a long-term view—and long-term relationships. Yet as partners, outsiders will get to know their clients very well over time; they will learn the industry and understand the organization and its leaders.

Consultants will work as business partners to link their efforts to their clients' human resource and development activities. They'll understand the hiring, development, and promotion philosophies of the firm, and they collaborate, when appropriate, on assessment, evaluation, and succession planning. They ensure that all of the efforts undertaken by the company are consistent with and linked as directly as possible to all other developmental activities.

True consultant-partners strive to become members of the leadership-development team, working closely to supply creative ideas, solutions, and support that will help the team meet its goals. They'll do more than simply bring an outside perspective to the table; they'll also share best practices from across the management and executive-development industry to ensure that their clients are leaders in the field.

Effective partnerships with outsiders extend beyond the parties involved. Indeed, a critical test of an outside consultant is the degree to which the firm will work directly (and cooperatively) with other client partners or providers. Here, they can be judged by both their words and their deeds. Rather than look for ways to criticize other providers, true consultant-partners welcome the opportunity to link those activities with theirs in order to create a seamless development strategy for the client.

Partnering is a natural outgrowth of the increasing emphasis on custom development of executive education. Understanding a company and its executives enough to deliver a customized program promotes increased efficiency and effectiveness for the organization, especially when spread across multiple programs. In fact, a tailor-made program from an outside consultant can prove to be a company's greatest leadership-development success.

To ensure that an organization's senior management is on board and aligned with the firm's developmental initiatives, there are two supporting interventions that are often helpful.

The Leadership Summit

A leadership summit is usually a one- or two-day working event to which the president, top executives, and other participants are invited by the CEO. This session is designed in a way that the senior leaders will:

▲ Engage in an activity that applies directly to the development, communication, and implementation of the firm's strategy. The output may lead to a major action-learning program (sometimes called The President's Leadership Challenge) and other leadership-development programs.

▲ Flesh out the firm's strategic imperatives as themes for high-level action-learning challenges and other leadership-development programs.

▲ Begin to develop messages that communicate the organization's strategy and leadership model. These messages form the core of communications efforts with the talent pool, leading up to other key leadership-development programs.

The goals of the leadership summit are four:

1. Articulate a strategy for leadership development throughout the organization.
2. Draw a big-picture design of the leadership-development program for the talent pool.
3. Craft the leadership messages that will communicate the firm's strategy—and its leaders' perspectives—to the talent pool via the high-potential and other leadership-development programs.

4. Prepare senior executives for their role as sponsors of the challenges to be given in action-learning or leadership-development programs.

Typically, the leadership summit is codesigned by an internal and an external team, but it is facilitated by an outside resource in order to avoid internal biases or straying beyond the agenda. It usually includes discussions and content sessions that focus on real work output, including articulation of the firm's leadership strategy. The leaders' main work during these sessions, however, consists of shaping the major initiative (often a high-potential action-learning initiative) and other leadership-development programs to ensure that they stress the firm's strategy and priorities. The leadership summit ensures that leaders own the leadership strategy and the key leadership-development programs. It also ensures that these leaders fully understand the purposes of the leadership strategy and the development programs. The leadership summit, then, establishes the role that senior executives will lead and notes their responsibility for development of the talent pool. It is intended that these executives both act on their major responsibilities and modeling the behavior for others in the firm.

The Communications Initiative

Through the communications initiative, group leaders articulate the vision, values, themes, perspectives, and frameworks that characterize the firm's direction and preferred future. The insights, commitments, and plans generated at the leadership summit are shared with all employees in the organization. Developing a plan to cascade that message down through the company's levels helps codify the plan. It also gives notice that "this is the direction we're taking." For example, Caterpillar rolled out its Vision 2020 program in late 2005 via sessions that cascaded down the organization. Or the method may be as simple as sending a detailed e-mail to all managers. Generally, a corporate newsletter, magazine, video broadcast, or all three are employed to get the message out.

It is essential that the talent pool hear these leadership-development messages clearly and consistently. They will then understand the case being made for business change, will translate and implement those changes at their levels, and will develop their own strategic actions in support of the plan. The communications-initiative design, then, begins at the leadership summit and continues through the crafting and delivery of messages to the talent pool.

The communications initiative is a critical element for creating the context for leadership development, and so it can (and should) include both internal and external communications.

▲ *Internal communications* should be coordinated, focused, and consistent. Beyond that, the effort should be sufficiently innovative to communicate the firm's leadership-development story to multiple constituencies.

▲ *External communications* should be aligned with strategy and internal messages. For example, articles and teaching materials might be circulated among leading business schools and corporate universities to call attention to the organization's leadership-building initiatives. This will enhance the organization's reputation as an employer of choice—and as an innovative company overall.

Successful Strategic Leadership Development: Summary

Implementing a leadership-development strategy that is to succeed requires that an organization address its own needs—and to do so, it must first understand them. Best-in-class leadership development is both intimate and organization-specific; as such, it requires internal knowledge coupled with some external refining. To be successful, all components of a talent-management system must be created with a single, ultimate goal. Happily, when all the components of a human-capital system are aligned, implementation becomes a natural outcome of these coordinated efforts.

Chapter 6 explores how the best-practice partners measure and evaluate the success of their leadership-development strategies. We also show how a successful leadership strategy impacts not only the human side of the business equation but also the business strategy and vision. But first, Chapter 5 looks at the special challenges and opportunities associated with leadership-developmental activities aimed at high potentials—and the potential these programs have to provide leverage for strategy.

Leveraging Leadership Development for High Potentials

We didn't plan to write a chapter on the development of high-potential employees. However, though we asked only a few questions about the topic during our research, we found that our best-practice partners placed significant emphasis on it. Consequently, we decided to look more carefully at our data, as well as data generated by other studies.[1] We found that the best firms place great emphasis on the development of high-potential employees and spend a great deal of money on this portion of the leadership-development challenge because they see the prospect of its having both immediate and long-term impacts.

A Focus on High Potentials

Key Finding 12. Corporate learning initiatives tend to focus on high potentials. Every CEO intuitively knows that developing the next generation of leaders makes good business sense. Several research studies confirm the value of this intuition.

▲ Organizations with strong leadership bench strength have approximately 10 percent higher total shareholder return than their weaker peers.[2]

▲ Companies with above-average financial returns have more comprehensive succession-planning processes and are more committed to developing future leaders.[3]

▲ Employees with strong leaders are more satisfied, engaged, and loyal than employees with weak leaders.[4]

▲ Comprehensive programs to develop high potentials can provide strategic leverage for corporate initiatives.[5]

Companies that identify and develop high-potential employees into executive leaders show solid shareholder returns. In 2005, Hewitt Associates conducted survey research involving 374 large U.S. companies and follow-up interviews with 75 of these firms to determine the top twenty firms for leaders. This research found that over a third of the firms (37 percent) did not use a consistent, formal approach to identifying their high-potentials. Among the top twenty firms, almost 80 percent had well-defined plans for identifying and developing high potentials. Firms with the highest total shareholder return (TSR) consistently had practices that connected pay and leadership-development activities to the careers of their high potentials. This suggests that to achieve consistent success, organizations must enforce an effective identification and development process that focuses on the desired traits and abilities needed in senior leadership positions.

The demand for new leaders is rapidly outgrowing the supply. As a result, most organizations are focused on identifying and cultivating those employees with the greatest potential to grow into business leaders. Yet surprisingly few organizations believe that they are doing this as effectively as they would like. A 2005 Corporate Leadership Council survey found that approximately three-quarters of companies worldwide are not confident in their ability to effectively staff leadership positions over the next five years. Moreover, a 2004 Conference Board report shows that only one-third of companies believe they are effective at identifying capable leaders early in their careers.

An Impending Leadership Crisis

There are several factors that suggest many organizations are heading for a leadership crisis. The following demographic and cultural trends are indicative of what is confronting senior line executives and human resource professionals charged with leadership development:

▲ *Departure of a Generation of Leaders.* The potential wave of retirements in the next ten years, led by the baby boomers, is of immediate concern. Born between 1946 and 1964, many people will turn sixty-five within the next five years. Over the next twenty-five years, about 80 million employees will retire.

▲ *From Boom to Bust.* The generation that follows the baby boomers has 20 to 25 percent fewer people, and so there may not be enough leaders to fill all vacant executive positions. By the year 2020, an overwhelming majority of today's senior leaders will have retired. At the same time, corporate growth plans suggest that firms will need to hire leaders into as many new positions as they currently have— while still replacing the leaders who have retired or left the company.

▲ *Decline of Leader Loyalty and Organizational Commitment.* According to the National Guidance Research Forum, the present generation of professionals is expected to change jobs about fifteen times during the course of their careers. Although job changes can be developmental for the individuals involved, they still result in a loss of talent for the organization.

▲ *Loss of Knowledge and Social Capital.* More retirements and high turnover rates translate into a loss of the company-specific knowledge acquired during these executives' careers, as well as loss of each departing executive's social network.

▲ *Increasing Technical and Global Complexity.* Globalization and the spread of technology have made it impossible to conceive of leadership talent in nontechnical and nonglobal terms, necessitating more time and developmental assignments to develop the desired talent.

Developing high-potential employees into effective leaders is more important than ever. Rapid economic growth, the likely loss of leadership talent owing to retirement, and the increased complexity of business operations owing to regulation, globalization, and other factors make it imperative that organizations identify and nurture the talent inherent in their ranks. Doing so can encourage retention, increase productivity, and create a talent pool for the senior ranks. The aforementioned trends are contributing to costly gaps in the flow of qualified talent rising to lead corporations or lines of business. From the retirement of experienced managers to the movement of service jobs overseas, the pool from which companies can pull able and ready high-potential leadership talent appears to be shrinking.

Although 75 percent of those companies polled said grooming high-potential workers for leadership is a top priority for both the CEO and human resources department, 97 percent also said that there continue to be significant gaps in their leadership talent pool. The majority of respondents said that such a shortage has a negative impact on a company's product innovation, ability to attract and retain talent, financial performance, and customer relationships.

As organizations evolve, executive-development program priorities may change or be reshuffled. A Human Capital Institute poll found the following major purposes for their high-potential programs: ensure bench strength/replacement for key jobs (79 percent), accelerate development of high potentials (62 percent), communicate vision and strategy to create alignment (61 percent), support organizational change and transformations (56 percent), develop capabilities of individual leaders (53 percent), and address key business issues/challenges (48 percent).[6]

High potentials are typically identified in their thirties or after five to eight years of employment. Consequently, the CEO who will be leading your firm in 2020 should already be on your radar screen as a member of the high-potential cadre. If a firm is not consciously nurturing the development of those individuals who will lead the organization in the next generation or so, it may be due for a vision exam.

Create a High-Potential Talent Pool with 2020 Vision

Companies that invest in promising workers often complain of only modest returns on their investments and moderate success at creating a high-potential talent pool. But by examining the leadership-development process, from needs analysis to practices to outcome assessment, we are able to identify what is or is not working and why.

Linking High-Potential Leadership Development to the Business Strategy

The organization has to believe that developing high-potential employees—and communicating its importance clearly throughout the organization—is a basis for business success. Both research and common sense support this belief, but the effective implementation of this wisdom exceeds the level of knowledge. Perhaps a starting place for successful implementation is to work to understand what is required of high-potential employees to meet the leadership challenges of the next decade. These talented individuals' abilities need to correspond with the emerging leadership needs of the future to ensure that the talent pool supports the company's overall strategy.

Senior management and HR professionals typically create alignment through an implicit, if not explicit, needs analysis: Where is the organization going and why? What work needs to get done to get there? What are the current and future roles for senior executives in this process? What competencies (knowledge, skills, and attitudes) will the organization require of its future leaders? What leadership competencies does the organization currently have? What are the current gaps in the leadership competency continuum? What will be the future gaps? How do we attract, develop, and retain people to close these gaps?

It is this last question that defines each organization's leadership-development challenge. Intentions to hire the "best and the brightest" or seek out and hire only the "best corporate athletes" may do little to actually enhance the talent pool—even if an organization is successful in realizing these intentions—if talent selection and development do not fill the organization's competency gaps. This would be akin to hiring the best gymnast for a race.

Effective talent selection is not the sole success factor for businesses of the future. Caterpillar's succession-planning process begins with a definition of a future leader. This definition is based on the identification of twelve leadership competences, each grouped as pertaining to vision, execution, or legacy. In addition to using a competency model to govern the succession-planning process, Caterpillar requires that candidates for senior positions demonstrate the following characteristics: performance, diversity and inclusion, values in action, employee engagement, cross-functional experience, Six Sigma experience, global experience, and external experience (when applicable).

Involving Senior Leadership in Leadership Development

There's little doubt that effective leadership development is positively correlated with business success. Yet, the 2006 Human Capital Institute poll found that only a slight majority (56 percent) of respondents were satisfied with top management's level of involvement in leadership development.[7] More than a third of respondents reported that management's involvement was "not at all satisfactory." If top management's level of involvement is less than desired by those responsible for talent development, it is likely that the senior executives' implicit needs analyses or intuitive judgments of competency gaps are not integrated with the leadership-development process.

Companies that have the best leadership-development programs follow strategies that include:[8]

▲ A high-profile talent-management conference or leadership summit that links strategy and talent development

▲ A curriculum of education or action learning for key transition points

▲ Coaching of senior executives to allow them to practice leading as teachers

▲ Requests to the board to meet and assess rising stars

▲ A comprehensive plan for accelerating development

▲ Alignment and linkage of talent development and other HR initiatives to business strategy

Although the aforementioned ideas are not new, they are not widely practiced. Integrating these techniques with business strategy makes a firm best-in-class achievement.

Identifying Potential Future Leaders—Entering the Talent Pool

Relative to their peers, highly effective leaders tend to advance more rapidly and achieve better results. To identify these leaders formally, managers must communicate, use effective methods of assessment, and compare their results with known criteria associated with specific leadership levels.

A disciplined succession-management program offers many guidelines that can assist organizations in the design and implementation of a system for identifying high-potential employees. Consider the following succession-management practices as a starting point for high-potential talent identification:[9]

▲ Set specific time objectives for accomplishing targeted development actions.

▲ Allow flexibility to adapt to changing strategic needs.

▲ Share information with candidates involved in succession planning.

▲ Include senior executives involved in identifying and developing candidates. Make their involvement and support visable throughout the organization.

The ongoing tasks involved in identifying, tracking, and developing high potentials in an organization requires concerted thought, extensive effort, and ongoing supervision of the talent. Clear communication regarding a high-potential program is best for all those involved in talent identification. The majority of organizations studied seem to keep talent identification somewhat secret from the board and the high-potential talent itself.

There are conflicting opinions regarding the benefit of informing employees of their high-potential status. Informing employees of their high-potential status sends a powerful message that the company values their contributions and believes in them enough to invest in their future. There is the risk that, if not told, the employees will move on to organizations that do recognize and develop their talents. High-potential employees generally know their potential and how they are viewed, whether they are officially told or not. As one HRD executive commented, "If they don't figure out that they are high potentials, maybe they aren't." In defining the criteria for high-potential employees, an increasing number of leading firms link the identification of talent to current job performance rather than rely exclusively on an inventory of attributes and new skills believed to be needed in future leadership positions. Some best-practice firms use their competency models and 360-degree performance feedback to identify talent. PepsiCo alternates between using multirater feedback one year and data from the firm's climate survey the next as part of the appraisal process.

In the identification of high potentials, a focus on current performance should be coupled with clear criteria that evaluate and measure future potential. All of the best-practice firms in the 2005 and 2006 APQC studies used some version of a matrix to assess talent on the basis of both performance and future leadership potential.[10] This hybrid approach should not only increase the quality of the talent pool but also provide indicators of success as individuals advance in their careers. Moreover, by identifying talent on the basis of current and desired skills, organizations develop greater confidence in their high-potential employees and tend to measure success with greater accuracy.

In addition to identifying current employees for their high potential to fill senior management positions five to ten years in advance, many companies hire high-potential talent into the organization at midmanagement levels, sometimes using executive search firms to source and screen viable candidates. An alternative to using search firms is to hire external talent already known to the organization's leaders from past relationships, such as the top talent at external service providers (business consultants, lawyers, accountants, public relations specialists) or co-workers at a previous employer.

The hiring of consultants into midlevel ranks has become sufficiently common so that all of the major consultancies have alumni programs that track the progress of their ex-employees and partners as they rise in the corporate world and target them as contacts to sell additional consulting services. Companies such as PwC, McKinsey, and Booz Allen Hamilton actively promote their extensive and high-profile alumni network to recruits and new hires. By placing employees into the middle echelon of the corporate hierarchy, companies reduce the amount of time and developmental activities necessary for them to excel.

Manage the Talent Pool

There are two general categories of high-potential employees: late-stage midcareer hires, and early career hires. Late-stage high potentials include experienced managers and professionals ready to make their way into the executive ranks. This group of middle- to senior-level staff can include new employees brought in to address perceived internal deficiencies and longstanding employees who have successfully negotiated earlier developmental challenges. Late-stage high potentials are likely to participate in a moderate amount of educational programming, with extensive amounts of specialized mentoring, executive retreats, personal coaching, real-world action learning, and global job rotations. These late-stage high potentials are among the top 5 to 10 percent of an organization. Significant costs are incurred to prepare them for the next level of executive challenges.

Most leadership-development programs support the need for leaders to obtain feedback from others on their skills (e.g., 360-degree assessments, decisions, and outcomes resulting from those decisions).[11] Obtaining such assessments and feedback in a timely and productive manner is becoming increasingly important to talent assessment. More often than not, only limited stakeholder feedback is solicited by leaders or their organizations. Unsolicited feedback is frequently viewed as critical rather than developmental. Such feedback can lead employees to be defensive and resistant to learning and professional development. To preclude defensiveness and enhance employees' openness to learning, senior leaders must be proactively involved with their key stakeholders in the discussion of talent development.[12]

Different Types of Management

Early stage high potentials differ from late-stage ones. These new managers and individual contributors are at an early stage in their careers and are identified more by their potential and drive than by past performance. Early stage high potentials are found in the middle ranks of an organization. Their employers are generally not yet ready to invest heavily in their formal training and development. Historically, organizations have focused primarily, if not entirely, on late-stage high potentials. Today, however, more organizations are adopting aggressive programs for developing bench strength throughout the organizational hierarchy.

Top-performing organizations especially recognize that the sooner potential talent is identified and developed, the sooner the organization reaps the rewards associated with more effective leadership. Both human resources and business line managers should be involved in the talent-identification process to ensure that assessments reflect both empirical data on performance and the organization's ideological criteria and vision.

Success should be linked to rewards. Firms that showed the highest shareholder return frequently link compensation to a leader's future potential. As shown in Figure 5.1, for the top companies surveyed, the organization's leadership competencies were tied to succession planning and reward systems. In the 2005 Hewitt study as well as the 2006 APQC project, succession planning was universally practiced by the best-practice firms and by a majority of the comparison companies. Linking competency development to base pay, annual incentive pay, and long-term incentive pay was much more common for the top companies than for the comparison firms.

What Needs to Take Place in the Talent Pool

Once its goals for high-potential programs are clear, an organization needs to develop a sufficient number of early stage high potentials at a fraction of the annual budget for sourcing and developing late-stage

Figure 5.1. Leadership-development models aligned with performance and reward systems.

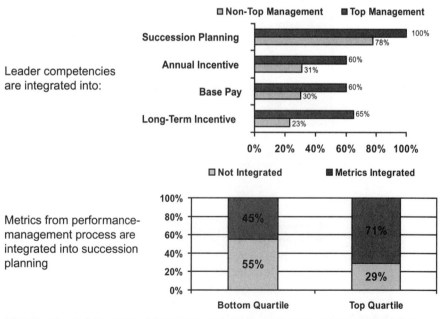

SOURCE: Michelle Salob and Shelli Greenslade, "How the Top 20 Companies Grow Great Leaders" (Hewitt Associates, 2005).

candidates for senior management. Results of research on techniques used to develop early stage high potentials are shown in Figure 5.2.

Providing access to senior management for high potentials is almost universal among the best practice firms, as are ample internal training opportunities and special development assignments. Mentoring and coaching for high potentials is done by a majority of the top companies, but by less than a quarter of the total. As illustrated in Figure 5.3, the best firms for leaders are typically twice as likely to use a variety of developmental techniques for "the best and brightest."

What these firms do isn't particularly unique. They just do more of it and do it more consistently. Many different techniques are used by progressive firms to develop high-potential talent. Figure 5.3 shows some of the most common themes found in our research, along with some interesting, but less common, practices. Some of the

Figure 5.2. Techniques used to develop high potentials.

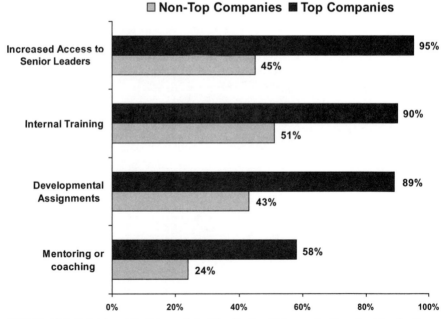

□ Non-Top Companies ■ Top Companies

- Increased Access to Senior Leaders: 95% / 45%
- Internal Training: 90% / 51%
- Developmental Assignments: 89% / 43%
- Mentoring or coaching: 58% / 24%

SOURCE: Michelle Salob and Shelli Greenslade, "How the Top 20 Companies Grow Great Leaders" (Hewitt Associates, 2005).

Figure 5.3. High-potential best-practices overview.

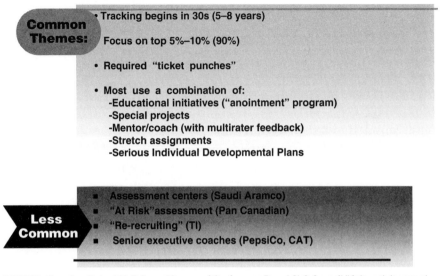

Common Themes:
- Tracking begins in 30s (5–8 years)
- Focus on top 5%–10% (90%)
- Required "ticket punches"
- Most use a combination of:
  - Educational initiatives ("anointment" program)
  - Special projects
  - Mentor/coach (with multirater feedback)
  - Stretch assignments
  - Serious Individual Developmental Plans

Less Common
- Assessment centers (Saudi Aramco)
- "At Risk" assessment (Pan Canadian)
- "Re-recruiting" (TI)
- Senior executive coaches (PepsiCo, CAT)

SOURCE: Based on Robert M. Fulmer, "Survey of Conference Board CLO Council," internal document, 2005.

more cost- and resource-efficient practices for implementing a successful early stage high-potential program include:

▲ *Specialized Leadership-Development Tracks.* As suggested previously, all of the firms identified as best-practice or top firms for leaders have programs in place to identify and provide special development opportunities for managers believed to have high potential. Less successful firms are less likely to have a well-developed program for high potentials and are also less likely to use the key techniques to accelerate development.

▲ *Developmental/Stretch Assignments.* Perhaps the most important tool for the development of high potentials is the rotation of managers across disciplines, divisions, and geographies. Top HRD professionals support the axiom that 70 percent of career development takes place on the job. Practically all of the best firms consciously espouse this axiom, broadening and stretching the most promising of their midlevel managers. Less than half of the comparison firms use rotational or developmental assignments as a regular component of their leadership-development efforts.

▲ *Specialized Learning Opportunities*. All of the 2006 best-practice firms report having specialized, highly customized, "by nomination only" leadership-development programs for their high-potential employees. These programs typically involve a heavy commitment by senior executives in the sponsorship and delivery of the program, often supplemented by facilitation and coaching by outside specialists. Limiting admission to these programs helps control costs and reserve coveted development opportunities for peak performers at critical stages in their careers. High-potentials tend to seek out and take advantage of opportunities for behavioral skill-building at a much greater pace than their peers. Consequently, top-performing organizations provide them with almost unlimited access to programs that accelerate their growth.

▲ *Leveraging Technology*. Because it is virtually ubiquitous, technology is more democratic than other developmental tools and is used in two ways by many firms. First, technology-enhanced learning improves leadership behavior on the job. The combination of synchronous and asynchronous tools and content, especially when paired with reinforced group application, can improve employees' performance at a fraction of the time and cost of classroom training. Typically, these technology-based programs are available to all interested employees. Yet, high potentials are more likely to use and benefit from them. Additionally, most firms use simple technology to allow all managers, but especially high potentials, to maintain up-to-date individual developmental plans (IDPs) that include relevant experiences as well as developmental targets.

▲ *Action Learning*. Because it brings development initiatives outside of the classroom and asks employees to solve real-world business problems, action learning is taking over as the learning organization's predominant, real-time, interactive simulation. In action learning, groups of high potentials and mentors are put into a situation and must solve a real, important challenge. Many organizations are migrating to this approach as a way to expand high potentials' perspectives on how their businesses operate. By offering a group of high potentials an educational program that provides a set of tools that might be used by outside consultants, and by asking high potentials to confront a corporate challenge of real significance, a firm can get an informed recommendation, provide a unique developmental experience for the participants, and embed the capacity for critical analysis and decision making in the organization. While action learning is typically associated with a specific learning initiative and accompanied by classroom time, high potentials may also be assigned to special projects or Six Sigma teams to address important issues and be observed by top management.

▲ *Coaching/Mentoring.* A majority of leading firms use internal mentoring programs to develop high-potential employees. Through pairing with internal senior mentors, high potentials are introduced to years of knowledge and experience. Leading firms use both internal and external coaches to address specific developmental needs (often revealed by multirater feedback) or to help action-learning groups as they grapple with complex challenges.

Some interesting, less common techniques we discovered in the current and previous research include:

▲ Pan Canadian's embrace of a concept of "at risk" assessment for reviewing high potentials who might be vulnerable to approaches from other employers because of a difficult boss, unpleasant assignments, or limited promotion prospects.

▲ Texas Instruments' use of a similar concept called "re-recruiting," in which special attention or perks were provided to outstanding managers who had not received a recent promotion.

▲ Saudi Aramco's use of an assessment center to provide feedback to large numbers of managers. The facility is especially useful in a culture in which providing constructive feedback is not a comfortable or common experience. At Saudi Aramco, the assessment process was also used to help identify candidates for the President's Leadership Challenge, an action-learning program for high potentials.

Case Studies of Talent-Development Systems

Despite having well-defined leadership attributes and leadership-development programs, many organizations may fall short of meeting their objectives. What follows are three corporate examples of integrated high-potential talent-development programs that seem to meet the objectives of their designers. These cases were collected as part of the 2006 benchmarking project discussed throughout this book.

PepsiCo's Talent Development

Recognizing that a large percentage of its executives will be eligible for retirement in the next several years, PepsiCo's senior leaders and HR team leverage a talent-development model to build bench strength at the executive level. PepsiCo's CEO program involves approximately forty high potentials each year. PepsiCo identifies individuals as high potentials during its people-planning process. Key questions for employees about this process include:

▲ *How do I get on a slate?* In addition to demonstrating functional expertise, an employee must also show a breadth of capabilities and experiences. Leadership skills take a high degree of importance in people-planning assessments.

▲ *How are selections made?* Every leadership job is filled from a list of well-qualified applicants. The majority of leadership jobs are filled by promotion from within the organization (this holds true for the CEO position as well). To be selected, an individual must be the most qualified person on the slate.

▲ *What happens at people-planning meetings?* A typical agenda includes discussion on organizational development, individual development, and bench development. Organizational-development discussions focus on progress against PepsiCo's key organizational-development and change-related initiatives such as inclusion goals. Organizational-health survey results provide important input into this review process. Individual-development discussions focus on the progress and development plans of individual executives. These discussions may include data from performance appraisals, 360-degree feedback, and other sources to enable conversation about how to help individuals grow. Bench-development discussions focus on talent differentiation, the leadership pipeline for key jobs, and staffing plans in the context of overall organizational plans.

In order to deliver on its model for sustainable advantage, PepsiCo needs a talent-management process that supports its two-pronged approach to building leadership capability: (1) offering broad-based tools that empower people to drive individual development in an inclusive and flexible work environment, and (2) aggressively building bench strength through experience planning for its future leaders. PepsiCo recently clarified its high-potential development process by updating its talent-development model to focus on three key components: identify, develop, and move. Each of the three elements of talent management focuses on certain tools and approaches. To develop readiness, the organization uses experiences, on-the-job training, coaching/feedback/mentoring, and formal training. The third component, movement, focuses on individual developmental needs that will allow employees to accumulate experience and contribute to the talent pool for the organization's senior-most roles.

A primary focus of PepsiCo's talent-management model at the executive level is on cross-divisional talent movement. To create a compelling vision for the future and to give teeth to leadership capability at PepsiCo, the HR organization realized that it needed to shift perceptions on the part of some senior leaders about how best to fill jobs. Figure 5.4 summarizes the older practices and the shift to current practices.

Caterpillar's Development Plan

As previously suggested, Caterpillar's succession-planning group works closely with the College of Leadership to provide high potentials with the experiences and opportunities needed to succeed. Development, performance management, succession management, and career planning are aligned with the Caterpillar Leadership Framework, which provides the core of the firm's leadership strategy.

Figure 5.4. Comparison of past and present development practices.

Past Practice (From)	New Practice (To)
Filling open jobs as needed	Creating thoughtful developmental opportunities to build bench strength
Promoting people to avoid turnover	Stretching the very best talent by giving them the experiences they need
Working with fair and predictable timelines	Differentiating and accelerating talent development where it makes sense
Keeping the best in your own backyard	Facilitating cross-divisional and cross-functional moves to ensure well-rounded future leaders
Stretching the best talent via piling on more work and fewer resources	Ensuring appropriate support and strong teams to achieve success for the business and the individual

For high-potential middle managers and above, Caterpillar's annual talent-assessment process involves the employee's manager and the business-unit management team. The conversation focuses on the individual's recommended next moves and what career experiences he or she needs. This is followed by an assessment of the person's long-range potential (ten years or more) and the employee's potential for future promotions.

Washington Group's Development Plan

Washington Group's Leadership Excellence and Performance (LEAP) project began in 2002 and graduates approximately twenty participants per year. It focuses on high potentials who show leadership promise. The program provides individual feedback and action plans, 360-degree assessments, and exposure to a variety of experiences in its six business segments. Each participant is also assigned a sponsor from the executive team. Participants have the opportunity to meet with board members as well as to shadow the CEO.

Another program for Washington Group is its Leaders Forum. This program targets senior-level high-potential managers and professionals who show leadership promise and the ability to move into more responsible positions. The Leaders Forum is a cornerstone of the leadership-development process. It is a fifty-six-hour course that was first offered in February 2004. More than 475 participants have attended one of the nineteen sessions to date. The course objectives are to:

▲ Develop the leadership capability of the organization

▲ Institutionalize the organization's mission and values as "the way we do business"

▲ Understand the organization's capabilities, markets, and competitive discriminators

▲ Value people as a strategic resource

▲ Understand and fulfill the role of leader in developing people

High-Potential Employee Development: Summary

Organizations cannot develop tomorrow's leaders with a fragmented approach. A substantial body of research and best-practice experience demonstrates the effectiveness of an integrated leadership initiative. Employees with high leadership potential need to be systematically identified and tracked by line managers as part of an overall strategic succession-planning process. Senior leaders and managers should articulate the major competencies required for leadership. In the best firms, senior leaders right up to C-level support high-potential programs by taking significant ownership over their success. Planning, implementation, monitoring, and review of leadership-development initiatives require the attention and effort of all elements of organizational hierarchy. All are important, but none offers greater leverage than developing the next generation of top leaders.

There are common attributes of potential leaders that cut across industries and may serve to differentiate future leaders from employees with less potential. Organizations are looking for talented people who demonstrate global thinking, cross-cultural awareness, ability to build alliances and partnerships, technological savvy, and belief in leadership sharing or people partnerships. Leaders who display a high level of energy, who show the ability to do what has to be done, and who energize others are always in high demand. As this book has shown, a company that truly understands the need for leadership planning now will have the leaders it needs tomorrow to remain competitive.

Most key corporate initiatives in this study focused on those individuals designated as high potentials within an organization. One reason for this is that these individuals have shown themselves to be open and receptive to these developmental programs. They are usually eager to take advantage of the opportunities given to them, recognizing them as a sign by the organization that great things may be in store for them. The knowledge and insights they gain are more likely to have a multiplier effect throughout the organization. Programs aimed at this constituency can provide a launching pad for major corporate initiatives. The challenges of implementing a strategic leadership effort will be explored in Chapter 6.

Evaluating Success in Strategic Leadership Development

If a tree falls in the forest and no one is there to hear it, does it make a sound? Many of us have considered this question philosophically; however, it really is a question of measurement. If we don't see, hear, or measure the results of an event, how can we be sure it really happened? How can we determine if a program successfully reached its intended outcome? The question of measuring the success of substantial investments in leadership development and other human capital development activities produces a great deal of concern and anxiety in corporations.

Corporations spend millions of dollars on training and development programs every year, including leadership-development programs. In fact, the best-practice partners in our study indicated that they spend a median of $8 million annually on leadership development. Of course, these organizations view this as an investment in their people and ultimately in their business models rather than an overhead cost. Still, given this high level of investment in leaders, is it surprising that organizations often have to justify this kind of spending? In fact, the pressure being placed on organizations to justify spending on employee development seems to be increasing. In a recent survey, 85 percent of human resource department respondents reported that assessment and evaluation will become more important over the next three years. Similarly, 88 percent agreed that "HR professionals will have to get better at proving the worth of executive education in the future."[1] In today's best-practice leadership-development companies, the drive to measure when the metaphorical tree falls, how and when it falls, and the impact of its fall has gained significant momentum.

The State of Assessment

Although the need to justify investments in leadership development is increasing, many companies are still quite unsophisticated in their assessment methods. In a recent survey, only 32 percent of respondents reported assessing their programs at level 5 according to Phillips's and Kirkpatrick's schemas[2] (see Figure 6.1), and only 22 percent had programs that were structured to be assessed according to return on investment (ROI). Similarly, just under half of the companies surveyed admitted assessing their learning results at level 4, which focuses on business impact and results.[3]

In another survey, Jim Bolt found that only 14 percent of respondents reported evaluating at level 4 (business impact/results), and half said they "seldom used" this level of measurement to gauge program success. Although 77 percent admitted extensively measuring participant reaction and satisfaction (level 1), only 18 percent and 19 percent, respectively, reported measuring learning of concepts (level 2) and application of concepts (level 3).

As we can see, the number of companies that thoroughly measure the impact of learning initiatives is surprisingly low despite substantial pressure to justify these investments. There are many reasons for this. First, as we've shown in this book, connecting an organization's

Figure 6.1. The great ambition of ROI measurement.

	Evaluation of Learning Results		
	% Using Each Level, Overall	Portion of Programs at Each Level	% Using Each Level, Expert
Level 1 (Reaction/Satisfaction)	90%	90%	94%
Level 2 (Learning of Concepts)	81%	55%	91%
Level 3 (Application/ Behavior)	70%	34%	82%
Level 4 (Business Impact/Results)	49%	26%	67%
Phillips Level 5 (ROI)	32%	22%	45%

SOURCE: "Sixth Annual Benchmarking Report," Corporate University Xchange, 2004.

learning strategy to its overall business strategy has many benefits, one of which is a natural ability to measure business results or the impact of a learning initiative. Many companies still operate with a learning strategy and methods that are disconnected from their overall business strategy, making rigorous assessment very difficult. Second, gaining access to appropriate data can be challenging, and creating a common language that defines value can also be difficult.

Finally, a barrier to measurement is often created by the mix of the program participants themselves. To maximize the gains from networking and collaborating across business units, learning professionals often construct programs of individual participants, rather than intact teams, selected from far-flung business units with differing roles and responsibilities. When these participants return to their jobs after attending an educational program, they can be quite isolated. Until a critical mass of program participants is achieved, these individuals cannot be expected to have a measurable business impact. In essence, an immediate benefit of the program—the opportunity for networking across businesses and job roles—creates a barrier for assessment.

Despite these barriers, some companies are quite innovative in their assessment practices. For example, IBM measured the impact of one of its largest management-development initiatives by creating business cases from participant interviews following the initiative. Not only did these cases qualitatively describe results, but they quantitatively documented the business impact of the program. Consulting firm Booz Allen Hamilton has pioneered the concept of value on investment, or VOI, as a measurement tool. Rather than using strict return-on-investment measures, Booz Allen incorporates institutional, participant, operational, financial, and strategic brand values to give a more holistic view of a program's impact. In essence, VOI measures the risk of not educating employees and considers all facets of business, including the operational, foundational, financial, and strategic. This type of assessment is used only for company-wide initiatives, however, rather than individual programs, because it is so difficult to remove one event from a learning curriculum and determine a meaningful impact. Booz Allen presents the results of these assessments at the firm's "People Day," where employees engage in facilitated discussions on their development and the firm's investment in learning.[4]

Some of the commonly used measures of business impact include improved product/service quality, customer service, and sales efficiency; reduced operating costs; increased revenue and profits; and improved sales efficiency. As a further example, Accenture, a leading professional services firm, believes it is possible to measure the impact of a company's learning programs by focusing on just three tangible components: recruitment, productivity, and retention. It uses these three exclusively to measure business impact.

Moving Forward

Measuring the impact that strategic leadership development has on the organization helps the human resource department understand if it is spending its dollars in the right way (i.e., on the right learning activities) and at the right time (i.e., at the appropriate career transition). Among our study's participants, the types of measures used and the data collected varied from organization to organization. Some organizations calculated a return on investment (ROI) figure, while others were content with measuring participants' satisfaction and reaction levels. Which types of measures were used depended on the culture of the organization and its top management.

Our study revealed a trend among the best-practice partners of increasingly viewing "developing people" as a measure of executive success. This was a constant among these firms and seemed to differentiate them from the study's sponsors. Another trend that emerged was viewing the ROI of learning in terms of corporate success, or business impact, rather than individual performance. This chapter examines these trends more closely, as well as discusses how these organizations view leadership development as a process or journey rather than as a one-time event.

Measuring Success

> **Key Finding 13.** Developing people is a growing measure of executive
> success.

The best-practice partners we studied believe that people development is the best indicator of organizational success, especially into the future. PepsiCo has moved to compensate its executives for people development and now uses an equal allocation of incentive compensation for people development and business results.

Caterpillar found that its managers performed better at the execution and vision portions of the company's leadership framework than at the legacy or the developmental set of behaviors. Consequently, Caterpillar has focused on legacy in its learning programs. The College of Leadership uses its Employee Opinion Survey Leadership Index to assess how well its business leaders are displaying the leadership behaviors being promoted by the company.

PwC created a developmental program for its primary reporting partners (PRPs) to increase their people-development skills and mindset. The PRP is generally the person to whom a partner reports (i.e., a leader of the partner's product or industry group or an office leader within the partner's geography). This individual acts as both evaluator and coach to other partners and is a major component of the firm's people-development success. To increase chances for success in developing partners, the firm requires that every PRP attend the program. It also provides each PRP with a personal coach to facilitate the difficult conversations that the role involves.

Two of the three recent, essential changes Cisco made to its leadership-development philosophy include changing the focus of leaders from achieving technical and business results to achieving excellence in leading people and developing talent. These changes were accomplished through the use of "experience, exposure, and education" (taken from one of Cisco's two leadership frameworks) and by shifting from the sole use of learning events to a more holistic view of development.

For those managers at Washington Group who are eligible for incentive compensation, 30 percent of that compensation is determined by how well they develop their people. To further reinforce the importance of this activity, "developing people" will become a standard element in all managers' Development Planners (as the performance appraisal process is known) in 2007. Success will be measured accordingly.

The Measurement Process

The majority of best-practice partners (60 percent) have developed and currently use some sort of formal system for measuring the outcomes of their leadership-development strategies. Only 19 percent of the sponsor organizations do the same.

When asked how frequently they measure the success of their leadership-development strategies, best-practice organizations responded that they measure "when it makes sense to do so." Figure 6.2 indicates that the best-practice partners usually measure results annually and upon the conclusion of programs.

As shown in Figure 6.3, best-practice partners indicated that, when assessing the impact of their leadership-development programs, their primary concerns were behavioral change, impact on the business or organization, and participant satisfaction. Assessment by best-practice partners contrasts sharply with that of sponsor organiza-

Figure 6.2. How often do you measure the results of your leadership-development strategy?*

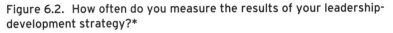
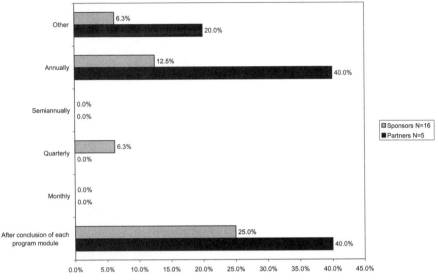

*Responses do not add up to 100% as respondents were asked to "check all that apply."

Figure 6.3. Which of the following are used to measure results of your leadership-development strategy?

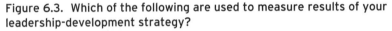
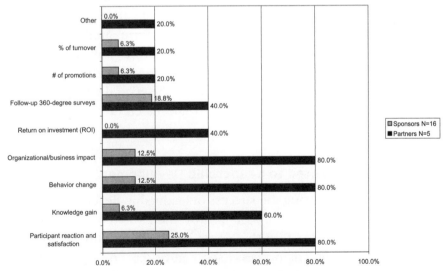

tions, which have not yet determined the best way to evaluate the success of their leadership-development programs.

Why are the aforementioned outcomes so important to the best-practice partners? It is important to understand the kind of impact that participation in these programs has on the individual and on the organization in order to better understand the following:

▲ The program's relevance (i.e., Is it meeting business needs? Is it aligned with business strategy?).

▲ Whether the budget for leadership development is being spent effectively.

▲ If the program is resulting in actual behavioral changes among participants.

▲ Whether participants are satisfied that the program is meeting their development needs.

Figure 6.4 notes some of the ways the study's best-practice partners calculated and collected these measures.

As we noted earlier, the types of measures used and how they are calculated vary from organization to organization. For some, Kirkpatrick's level I and level II measures suffice.[5] For others, a more thorough analysis (e.g., Brinkerhoff's Success Case Method) of the program's impact on the individual and his or her ability to be successful (and therefore make the organization successful) is required.[6] The decision as to what type of measure was used and what data were collected was connected to the organization's culture, as well as to the desires of top management.

The Impact Attributed to Leadership Development

Impact is key in assessing the success of leadership-development programs. When asked what major improvements or changes had occurred in their organization that could be attributed directly to their leadership-development process (see Figure 6.5 on page 112), the top five responses of the best-practice partners were:

Figure 6.4. Types and method of measurement.

Type of Measure Used	Measurement Calculation	Collection Method
Participant reaction and satisfaction	Quantitative and qualitative	Post-class questionnaire
	Averages	Level 1 evaluations
	Kirkpatrick Model (level 1)	Electronic survey
	Self-determined scores of 1–5	E-mail questionnaire
Behavior change	Qualitative	Observation and feedback; Success Case Method; various assessments on mind-set shifts
	Kirkpatrick Model (level 3)	Interviews about behavioral change
	Qualitative observation	Senior leaders' input about their people
Organizational/ business impact	Qualitative	Observation and feedback; Success Case Method
	Kirkpatrick Model (level 4)	Interviews to identify results achieved
	Scores of 1–5 on items, including trust in and connection to leadership	Company-wide semiannual survey ("pulse") results

1. Change in employee behavior

2. Improved collaboration and networking across organizational boundaries

3. Improved knowledge transfer across business units and among leaders

4. Improved reputation of the company

Figure 6.5. What major improvements or changes have occurred in your organization that can be attributed directly to the leadership-development process?

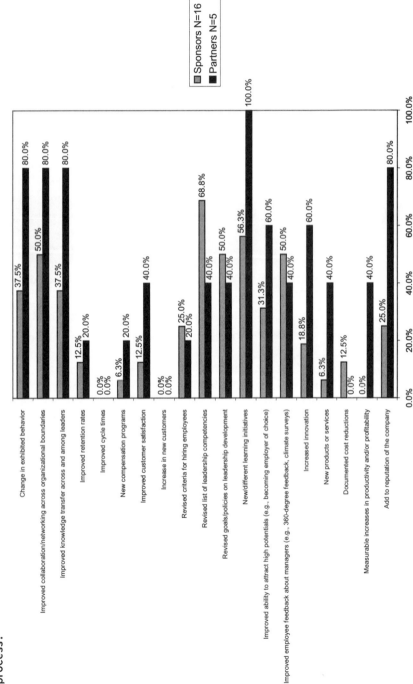

5. New or different learning initiatives

Although responses from the study's sponsors indicate an inward focus on leadership-development programs (e.g., a revised list of leadership competencies, new and different learning initiatives, and revised goals and policies on leadership development), the best-practice partners' top responses indicated that they looked both internally and externally for the impact of learning initiatives. In addition to observing internally focused results such as changes in behavior or improved collaboration, partners also looked for externally oriented results such as improvements in the reputation of the company. Many of the best-practice partners believe their leadership-development programs provide the organization with a competitive advantage, enabling it to maintain or improve market share as well as attract top talent.

Defining a Return on Learning

Key Finding 14. Return on learning is increasingly measured by corporate success rather than individual performance.

All of the best-practice partners were familiar with Kirkpatrick's and Phillips's models of evaluation. However, Caterpillar was perhaps the most rigorous in attempting to measure the return on investment in learning—which the company refers to as return on learning (ROL). Figure 6.6 details the framework Caterpillar uses to assess the success of its leadership-development efforts.

To help in the assessment of its programs, Caterpillar University created a document called the "Business of Learning." As part of the creation of this document, each college developed a value proposition for each key learning initiative based on net benefits, ROL, and other standards. The creation of the document was followed by a series of ROL studies. In these studies, Caterpillar identified the tangible and intangible benefits, costs, and ROL of learning initiatives. These benefits were then tied to improvements in productivity and quality

Figure 6.6. Caterpillar's learning evaluation framework.

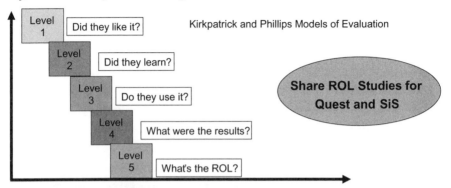

Metrics that matter

- An automatic learning-evaluation system, integrated with other Caterpillar learning systems
- Data collection, storage, processing, and reporting

or reductions in cost. According to Chris Arvin, dean of the College of Leadership (and a former accountant), the real benefit of these studies lies not in the numbers but in the ability to understand what people (e.g., program participants, executive sponsors) see as the true value of learning. In addition, these studies helped the organization do the following:

▲ Understand the costs and benefits of investments in learning

▲ Ensure that benefits are greater than costs

▲ Ensure that the ROL percentage compares favorably with other investments

▲ Understand how to reduce costs and increase benefits

▲ Encourage process owners and leaders to focus on the importance of participation and application

▲ Manage program deployment for success (achieve the target ROL)

▲ Use the benefit calculations to aggregate the impact of learning

To further its assessment focus, Caterpillar studies estimated ROL and forecasted ROL (when piloting a program) and also conducts a post-ROL assessment. Even after these substantial efforts, Arvin maintains that the actual ROL number itself is less important than the act of getting to the number. Arvin admits that the numbers are only approximations, and after the exercise of determining ROL is complete, the College of Leadership tends to emphasize participant comments. These comments are collected immediately after a program and then again six months after the program. In this survey, participants are asked to articulate what they are doing differently as a result of attending the program in question.

PepsiCo does not attempt to measure the value created by a leadership-development program. However, the CEO attends each program and serves as the program's primary facilitator. She is also intensely involved with program design and delivery. This level of executive involvement opens unique avenues for PepsiCo to do program assessment and follow-up. For example, at the end of each program, the CEO asks each participant to send her an e-mail indicating what he or she will be doing differently as a result of attending the session. Then, six months after the program has concluded, participants are again asked to send another e-mail reporting how thoroughly they have fulfilled their commitment.

Cisco collects both quantitative and qualitative measures of program success. Its Worldwide Leadership Development unit has a formal system for measuring the outcomes of leadership-development strategy. Examples of the metrics Cisco uses include price range for a one-week course, customer satisfaction scores, percentage of class graduates who have used information learned in their jobs and had a positive impact, and percentage of learners who stay with the company. After the data are collected, Cisco celebrates cases in which participant satisfaction is high and costs are low. However, the company also realizes that program participants might be satisfied with a course that yielded no positive business impact. Therefore, the Worldwide Leadership Development team concentrates on metrics that illustrate the application of participants' learning to their jobs, as well as to business results.

For two years, Cisco's Worldwide Leadership Development group used Robert Brinkerhoff's Success Case Method to measure the impact of its various programs.[7] The method uses case examples and stories from individuals to describe the best and worst in employee training and development and can also be used to quickly estimate return on investment.[8]

The method begins with the creation of an impact map (see Figure 6.7 for an example) that is designed to show what the organization needs to improve through leadership training—for example, customer satisfaction, growth, market share, and profitability. In order to evaluate results, the Worldwide Leadership Development

Figure 6.7. Cisco impact map.

Key Content	Key Behaviors	Results	Impact
Mind-set	**Grow Business**	• A higher percentage of time devoted to developing my team	• Customer Satisfaction
• I must overcome change and complexity in Cisco's strategy to help my teams excel in execution	• Took action to improve Cisco's bottom line	• Increased focus on implementing my team's initiatives and goals	• Growth
	• Prioritized to focus team around Cisco strategies		• Market share
• My role as emerging leader is to translate strategy into meaningful goals and to drive action	**Grow Team**	• Improved my team's morale and productivity	• Profitability
• I plan and anticipate conditions and remove barriers so that people are set up for success	• Developed new strategies and approaches for leading others	• Improved collaboration related to customer needs	
	• Developed strategies that leveraged the core strengths of my team and Cisco		
Skill set	• Increased the ability to conduct honest and direct conversations and feedback sessions with my staff		
• Developing relationships based on authentic sharing, empathy toward others, and a shared view of reality	• Enhanced my ability to match the right person with the right role and provide the right support		
• Holding effective interactions with people from different cultures, geographies, etc.	**Grow Self**		
	• Conducted a courageous dialogue with someone back at the office		
	• Expanded and leveraged the network created in EmLP		

team first attempts to understand what needs to be accomplished for the program to achieve its desired impact. According to one team member, it is important that the organization think strategically about how the program will drive the behaviors that will then create business impact.

For Cisco's Emerging Leader program, the team assesses the results of the program using a simple survey of five to eight behavior-based questions that were developed in consultation with the Brinkerhoff team. This survey is administered both before the program and again six to nine months following the program. In this survey, 98 percent of the participants reported that the program helped them "deliver measurable, concrete business impact." For further validation, these results are corroborated with comments from interviews with the participants' managers, peers, and/or direct reports.

Of course, the ultimate test of any leadership development program's success is the degree to which the firm meets its strategic objectives. The chances of this happening are increased when leadership development is aligned with corporate strategy. Though leadership development will never be the sole cause of strategic success, it can and should be seen as a contributing factor.

Integrating the Program

Key Finding 15. Successful programs are a process rather than an event.

In the past, corporate education programs have been a disconnected series of events. Today, these programs are typically part of an integrated career-development system that is tied to the organization's strategic objectives with specific, actionable goals. They are seldom discrete one-week events and now often include team or individual applications.

An example of this level of integration is the Cisco Leadership Series, which operates in a three-phase structure and facilitates the employee's ability to put learning into action (see Figure 6.8). The series follows an events-to-process model and allows participants to

Figure 6.8. Cisco leadership series, three-phase structure.

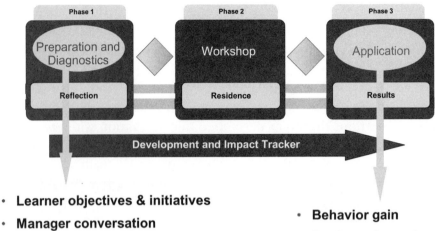

- **Learner objectives & initiatives**
- **Manager conversation**
- **Self-directed learning**

- **Behavior gain**
- **Business impact**

progress through each phase of the series. While the actual program lasts only a week, participants are deeply involved in the learning process for three to six months. The three phases of the series are as follows:

Phase 1—*Preparation*. Participants go through prereadings, diagnosis of their current level, and reflection. Through self-directed learning and conversations with their managers, learners become clear on their objectives for the program.

Phase 2—*Residential*. Participants participate in workshops, networking events, and activities, building upon their development in phase 1.

Phase 3—*Application*. Participants return to their jobs to apply their knowledge.

The first two phases lead to application. All phases are designed to focus on behavior change and business impact. The design team understands the behaviors it expects to change or improve when it designs the programs and tracks the impact of the programs accordingly.

PricewaterhouseCoopers designs its leadership programs with career progression in mind. Each program addresses a specific point in an employee's career journey or ladder. The foundation of each of these programs is the firm's values and strategy, leadership competencies, and strategic links (i.e., coaching initiative, pulse survey, and being a "great place to work"). This series of programs is called "The Backbone." Its focus on values and strategy provides continuity among programs, creating a process rather than a series of independent events.

Caterpillar's core leadership programs use key transition points in its leaders' careers. The programs occur as individuals move from supervisor (i.e., frontline leader) to manager (leader of leaders) to department head, and finally to executive. A person's movement through these programs and transitions is part of his or her developmental journey at Caterpillar. The core leadership programs also build on one another in a building-block fashion (see Figure 6.9). Underlying all of its programs is Caterpillar's foundational Making Great Leaders (MGL) program.

By envisioning and developing their programs as a part of a process rather than as a series of disconnected events, and by focusing on transition points in employees' careers, the best-practice partners leverage the key moments discussed in Chapter 1. Capitalizing on these moments of peak receptivity with employees increases the likelihood that desired effects such as behavior change and business impact will be achieved.

Assessing Success in Leadership Development: Summary

As the pressure to justify investment in learning and leadership development mounts, companies are looking for effective and innovative measurement methods, as well as practices that will increase the return on these investments. To improve return on investment, this study's best-practice partners emphasize the process of learning in

Figure 6.9. Building blocks of a core leadership program.

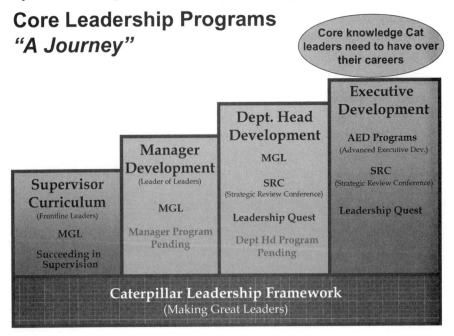

Core Leadership Programs
"A Journey"

multiple ways. First, they spend time with participants beyond the on-site portion of the learning program. Typically, participants are assigned prework before arriving at the program site. They may be asked to complete an online preparatory module to ensure they understand some portion of the actual program. Then, following the program, they are likely to be asked to focus on a particular challenge, meet with a coach, or report on their progress in fulfilling commitments made during the program. Supplemented by pre- and post-course work, programs become a process rather than a one-time event.

Second, leading companies in leadership development design educational programs around key transitions in a manager's career, further emphasizing the process nature of learning. These teachable moments tend to occur when an individual is asked to change his or her identity or mind-set in a new role: when an individual contributor first becomes a supervisor, when he or she becomes a manager of managers, or when the individual becomes a general manager with broader, bottom-line responsibility for an entire operation.

Finally, a growing trend among the best-practice partners is to view people development as a substantial measure of executive success rather than a nice by-product of other activities. Accordingly, people development has become a key component of performance scorecards and can represent a significant portion of an executive's compensation package. Though this trend seems to emphasize the individual's role in people development, a related trend is to determine return on learning overall by corporate success, rather than just by individual performance. Thus business impact and business results are what really matters when it comes to leadership development.

To ensure leadership development has significant business impact, this study's best-practice partners design their leadership-development strategies within the framework of the company's strategic needs and business context. Keeping these elements in mind during the design process helps ensure that the programs will (1) meet the business and development needs of program participants, and (2) achieve the desired business and strategic outcomes.

By following the aforementioned methods and focusing on assessment and business impact, the best-practice firms in this study have achieved strategic leadership-development initiatives that have delivered and will continue to deliver concrete, meaningful results to their respective organizations.

What's Next? The Future of Strategic Human-Capital Management

We know that great leaders deliver great results. Most important, companies that develop great leaders maintain a competitive advantage over those that do not. A company that can see into the future and develop leaders to meet its strategic needs will have a seemingly insurmountable advantage over its competitors that cannot. By documenting the leadership-development practices of some of the world's leading firms, we hope to have illuminated the connection between establishment of a clear leadership strategy and business success.

What did we see as we studied these best-practice partners? We saw organizations that embrace learning as essential to their business strategies and as a means of maintaining competitive advantage. We met leaders who understand the value of investing their time in teaching and learning, and who serve as an example in both. These same leaders are essential in establishing the value their organizations place on learning and have led the way in making leadership development and learning key elements of their business strategies. During our research, we were also introduced to leadership-development strategies and architectures that were wedded to overall business strategy. We met human resource leaders who understand the business as well as the theories and practices necessary to develop strong leaders. Finally, we saw innovations in the measurement of learning and development and an increased focus on people development as a measure of success and a determinant of reward.

The four main themes of this book and the fifteen key findings we have introduced here are summarized in Figure 7.1. But they do not represent amazing new technologies or concepts in leadership development; rather, they embody the fundamental elements of creating strategies, programs, and processes that will produce great leaders. Our best-practice partners were vigilant in implementing the techniques that lead to success. They are testament to our discovery that the best leadership-development companies emphasize and successfully execute the basics.

One could say that the best-practice partners in our study practiced the ABCs of effective strategic capital development by aligning learning and leadership development with corporate strategy, by maintaining a business focus in their development activities, and by collaborating and creating partnerships and connections with lines of business and processes such as corporate planning and strategy development. Alignment, business focus, and collaboration applied continually will create leaders who deliver great results. In essence, these practices offer the "inevitable surprises" that come from practicing the basics unfailingly.

The Future

It is important to look ahead to the future of strategic human-capital development. As a popular proverb suggests, "It is difficult to make predictions—especially about the future." Although it is impossible to predict the future conclusively, it is safe to assume that organizations that focus on leadership development will be more successful

Figure 7.1. Study's four themes and fifteen key findings.

1. Developing Leadership Strategy

    ■ *Organizations experience major change events leading to profound teachable moments.*
    ■ *Winning organizations build a strong linkage between business strategy and leadership-development strategy.*
    ■ *Executives use leadership development as a powerful tool to formulate, translate, and communicate strategy.*
    ■ *Lean competency models and values are the foundation of strategic leadership development.*

2. Building an Integrated Architecture for Strategic Leadership Development

    ■ *Strategic leadership development involves a conscious partnership between senior executives and multiple human resource systems.*
    ■ *Strategic HRD is a key part of the corporate planning cycle.*
    ■ *HRD can win the support of top management by involving it in strategic learning initiatives and by understanding the business.*
    ■ *Leaders who teach are more effective than those who tell.*

3. Implementing Successful Strategic Leadership Development

    ■ *HRD owns the process and maintains strategic control.*
    ■ *Lean human resource departments leverage their talents by partnering with outside experts.*
    ■ *Integration of leadership development with other talent-management systems creates valuable synergies.*
    ■ *Corporate learning initiatives tend to focus on high potentials.*

4. Evaluating Success

    ■ *Developing people is a growing measure of executive success.*
    ■ *Return on learning is increasingly measured by corporate success rather than individual performance.*
    ■ *Successful programs are a process rather than an event.*

than those that do not. We will continue to see companies that operate with lean competency models and activate these competencies in the daily work of individuals through real-time feedback, effective coaching, and evaluations that fuel development. These competencies will be visible and actionable for leaders and managers who are working as teachers and coaches with their employees and colleagues. But in the future, we will also see teams with built-in routines and processes that enable learning in the course of work rather than as a sideline, detached from the normal workday.

What do the aforementioned actions and philosophies suggest? We think they herald a return to the learning organization or, better yet, *the teaching organization.* In this type of organization, teaching and learning are valued and expected. In a teaching organization, leaders are actively involved in and lead the instruction through action and example rather than edict.

A learning culture can be described in a variety of ways, but generally coexists with a high-performance culture and accelerated development of human capital to maximize performance and drive sustainability. Establishing a learning culture will be the key to sustaining leadership development in the successful companies of the future. The learning culture—or teaching organization—will exhibit four key characteristics:

1. *It will see learning as a cultural value and process rather than a series of isolated events.* Learning organizations use both formal and informal instruction to develop and maintain a legacy of teaching and learning in the organization. They see knowledge acquisition and development as central to maintaining a competitive advantage and successfully executing their business strategy. They employ a wide range of educational methods, all driven by a clear focus on intended business outcomes.

2. *It will acknowledge the importance of sharing knowledge gleaned during the course of work.* Individuals in true learning cultures share several things in common. They see mistakes as opportunities to learn and to initiate systemic change. They avoid falling prey to stability traps and sacred cows by constantly challenging the status quo and questioning established norms. They proactively share information through informal personal exchanges, as well as through formal knowledge-sharing tools. These behaviors actually propel the continued development of new knowledge that can be embedded in products, services, and the organization's business model.

3. *It will align learning initiatives with business goals.* This phrase is a mantra we have chanted throughout the book. We see it

as gaining even greater importance in the future. Successful organizations actively create processes and structures that connect learning to business strategy and enhance specific capabilities. Organizations that align processes with strategies have high expectations and high standards for learning, capability development, and performance. As our best-practice partners show, lean competency models help employees understand, remember, and incorporate new information in their daily work. In a learning culture, competencies become embedded in the language of the organization, are observable and measurable, and are the benchmarks for judging performance.

4. *It will have a mature approach to leadership development that includes leaders who lead, teach, and respond to change with agility.* As illustrated by our best-practice partners, leaders in learning cultures are actively involved as teachers, mentors, and coaches. In addition, they help sponsor action-learning events and spend substantial time learning how to teach.

A focus on the above principles will facilitate the creation of learning cultures in the leading organizations of the future. Not only will people learn faster in these organizations, but leaders will develop more quickly. Organizations that do achieve a learning culture will focus on embedding learning and leadership development in the workplace, will institute team routines that apply learning and increase knowledge sharing and accountability at a local level, will operationalize competencies and make competency models a living tool rather than a list in a development handbook, will emphasize leaders as teachers and as role models, and will increase the return on their learning investment by making learning ubiquitous rather than something occasionally offered in a classroom at a remote conference facility far from the workplace. These learning-culture companies will not only have great leaders for the future but will have an advantage in the marketplace as well. In short, they will become the best-practice partners of the future.

PART II

Detailed Case Studies of Best-Practice Companies

Caterpillar University
College of Leadership

Site Visit Hosts:

- ▲ Chris Arvin, Dean, College of Leadership
- ▲ Deb Conklin, Succession Planning Manager
- ▲ Kim Converse, Senior Learning Consultant
- ▲ Pat Murphy, Manager, Succession Management
- ▲ Deb Nelson, Senior Learning Consultant
- ▲ Chris Schena, Vice President, Motion and Power Control Division
- ▲ Mary Seely, Human Resource Manager, North American Commercial Division

Organization Overview

Established in 1925 by Daniel Best and Benjamin Holt, Caterpillar is a global Fortune 100 organization with more than half of its sales outside of the United States. Caterpillar is the world's largest manufacturer of construction and mining equipment, diesel and natural gas engines, and industrial gas turbines. It is also a global technology leader in construction, mining, forestry, energy, logistics, and electric power generation. In 2004, the organization achieved a milestone of more than $30 billion in sales. In 2006, it had sales and revenues of $41.5 billion, up 38 percent from two years earlier.

Caterpillar produces more than 300 products that are sold in nearly 200 countries around the world. They are manufactured in almost 100 U.S. locations and 78 additional locations worldwide. These include track-type tractors, backhoe loaders, engines, paving products, wheel loaders, motor graders, excavators, off-highway trucks, and compact construction equipment.

Caterpillar currently employs more than 94,000 people worldwide; approximately 8,000 of those individuals are leaders (i.e., those who supervise others). By the year 2020, the organization will have hired 80,000 new employees due to growth and attrition. It is experiencing some rapidly changing demographics, with most of its employee growth in the next several years expected to occur outside the United States.

This summary focuses on Caterpillar University's College of Leadership (COL), which serves the entire Caterpillar enterprise. Caterpillar's senior management places a high priority on leadership development, and it is an area of increasing importance to the organization. Caterpillar University was established in January 2001 with an articulated enterprise-learning vision "to be recognized as one of the best continual learning organizations in the world." In addition to its recognition by APQC, Caterpillar University was ranked number 1 in 2005 by the American Society for Training and Development and it received similar recognition from Corporate University Xchange in 2006. Although our research was focused on the COL, led by Dean Chris Arvin, there are also Colleges of Marketing and Distribution; Caterpillar Production System; Technology; Six Sigma; and General Studies. Caterpillar University delivers its learning with an emphasis on enterprise-wide learning programs for classroom delivery along with collaborative efforts with the business units that focus on e-learning, knowledge sharing, leadership development, change management, and business acumen. Caterpillar University works in partnership with lead learning managers from each business unit for alignment and execution of enterprise learning goals. The lead learning manager is responsible for managing learning within the various business units. Lead learning managers and subject-matter experts also serve as advisers on key initiatives as part of global teams. The governance of Caterpillar University is headed by a board of governors that includes the CEO and senior executives who determine policy and approve learning budgets and priorities. Each college has an advisory board that includes senior leaders from the user groups. Members of each advisory board represent various business units as well as reflect geographic and subject-matter mix.

Developing Leadership Strategy

Over the past four years, the COL created the organization's leadership-development strategy. Several new leadership initiatives have been successfully deployed in that time. Each initiative:

▲ Is firmly linked to business goals

▲ Actively engages senior leaders in the design and teaching

▲ Is fully integrated with all other relevant people processes

▲ Is evaluated for application to the workplace and impact on the business

In addition to the strong links between leadership development and business goals, the leadership-development strategy has connections to the organization's culture and values. Caterpillar's enterprise strategy (Figure A.1) identifies people as a strategic goal and contains a "people" critical success factor (CSF) with metrics in leadership, learning, and diversity. The metrics are sourced from the annual employee opinion survey (EOS), which is administered to all employees for feedback. The vice presidents of Caterpillar's thirty business units

Figure A.1. Caterpillar's enterprise strategy.

are responsible for achieving an EOS index of 80 percent for leadership and 90 percent for engagement by 2010.

The alignment of enterprise with leadership strategy is interwoven in terms of both process and content. Caterpillar University attempts to ensure that learning is linked to business goals and critical success factors. Its focus is on the highest-priority learning areas where it can have the greatest impact. Caterpillar spends more than $100 million on learning but wants to be sure this is the "right learning." The Vision 2020 Enterprise Strategy was introduced in late 2005. Its creation was a product of a strategic-planning committee involving senior executives as well as high-potential leaders. Input was also provided from the integrative exercise in the firm's high-potential program, Leadership Quest. The rollout of this strategy demonstrated the firm's commitment to leaders as teachers, with 7,000 managers presenting the new strategy to 80,000 employees within a three-month period.

Each year the COL reaches out to the board of governors and lead learning managers in all thirty business units to assess learning needs for the following year. The college partners with these leaders to design, develop, and deploy high-impact leadership development globally.

Figure A.2 is an important summary of the COL's strategy. It begins with a statement of central purpose: "Long-term success by partnering to develop great leaders." The key steps required to embed the leadership strategy in the organization are then spelled out. Note that these steps include specific ties to the business, the promotion of individualized learning, and the emphasis on leaders who "teach, coach, and learn." The key metrics and priorities for the coming year are also identified to make the strategy more concrete and actionable.

At Caterpillar, responsibility for the leadership-development strategy is shared between Caterpillar University and each of the thirty business units. For example, Caterpillar University has responsibility for conducting needs analysis, developing leadership programs, and maintaining the leadership framework, whereas the lead learning manager of the business unit is responsible for developing a division

Figure A.2. College of Leadership Strategy.

College of Leadership Strategy

Our Purpose The reason we exist	Our Key Steps How to embed Leadership	Our Success Profile What success looks like	Our Key Actions What we will do in 2006
Supporting Caterpillar's long-term success by partnering to develop great leaders. **Living by...** OUR VALUES IN ACTION	1. Executive sponsorship with tie to the business 2. Create & embed a foundation of leadership knowledge 3. Promote individualized learning 4. Apply learning (do, reflect, connect) 5. Build leaders who teach, coach & learn 6. Measure success & hold leaders accountable	*Lagging Metrics* • $50B in sales • EPS growth top half of S&P 500 (2005-2010) • 80% engagement index • 80% leadership index • Leadership pipeline full *Leading Metrics* • BU call us first, a partner • All leaders have and act on development plans • Framework integrated • Key leadership transition programs in place (e.g., Supv, Mgr, DH) • Externally recognized	• Deploy MGL to mgrs • Design MGL for supv • Integrate leadership framework with Values in Action • Deploy SiS • Design and deploy dept head program • Deploy Quest • Deploy LBL • AED program • Executive coaching • Deploy e-learning • Consult with BUs

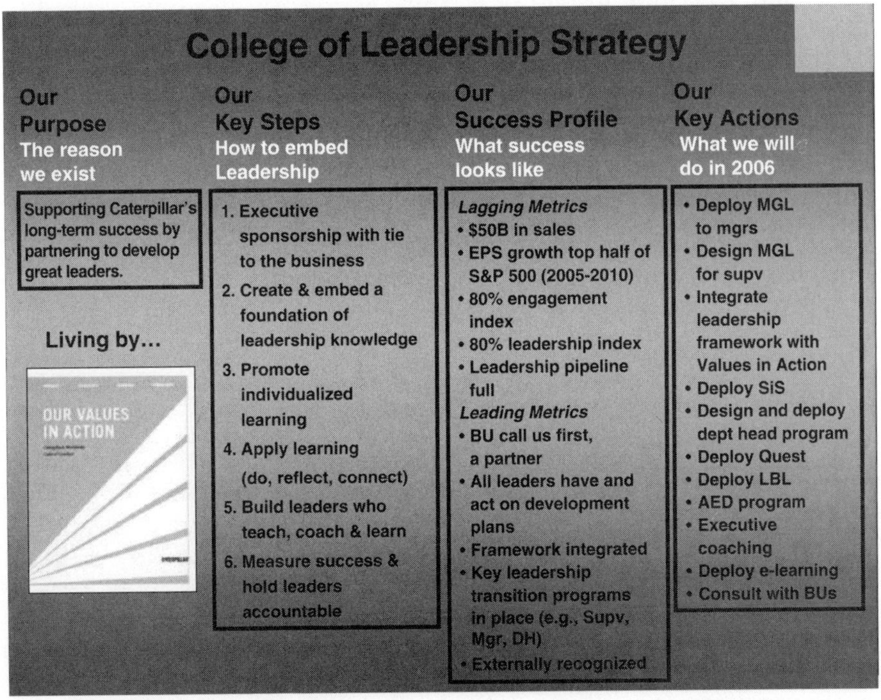

learning plan (a proactive forecast of the learning and development programs needed for the next year).

Building and Implementing an Integrated Leadership Roadmap

Caterpillar's Leadership Framework is linked to the organization's core human resources processes, such as selection, development, performance management, succession management, and career management. For example, The Caterpillar Leadership Competencies are currently being integrated into the targeted selection and performance-management processes. Additionally, Caterpillar's new global succession-management process includes discussion on these competencies as well as a three-year EOS leadership index trend. This integration is illustrated in Figure A.3.

Caterpillar's Leadership Framework

Successful implementation of learning initiatives and their contribution to the overall objective of developing leaders is coordinated within every aspect of the human resource system. Specifically, learn-

Figure A.3. The Caterpillar leadership framework.

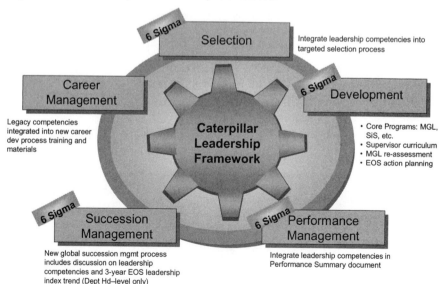

ing initiatives take into account and are built around developmental needs associated with Caterpillar's leadership competencies. Working with an outside partner, Caterpillar collected information from leaders in the organization regarding the anticipated requirements for future success. Expert panels and strategic interviews were connected along with a benchmarking review of executive competences used by other organizations. After analyzing the collected data, a set of competencies reflecting the Caterpillar organization was developed. These are shown in Figure A.4. On the left side of this chart, competencies associated with managers and supervisors are outlined, while the right side features executive leadership. Although many leaders might have trouble reciting all of the competencies, almost every manager in the organization would know the importance of having vision, the means for execution, and leaving a legacy.

The Journey Through Key Career Transitions

The Caterpillar Leadership Framework is a key component of a core program that CAT has developed with the Hay Group, called Making

Figure A.4. Defining leadership competencies at Caterpillar.

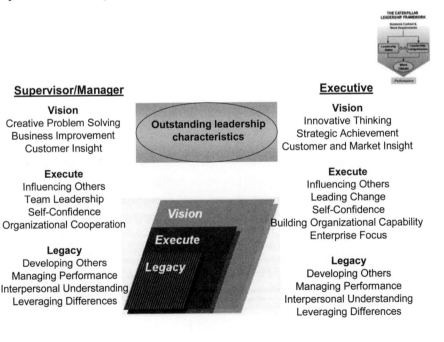

Supervisor/Manager

Vision
Creative Problem Solving
Business Improvement
Customer Insight

Outstanding leadership characteristics

Executive

Vision
Innovative Thinking
Strategic Achievement
Customer and Market Insight

Execute
Influencing Others
Team Leadership
Self-Confidence
Organizational Cooperation

Execute
Influencing Others
Leading Change
Self-Confidence
Building Organizational Capability
Enterprise Focus

Legacy
Developing Others
Managing Performance
Interpersonal Understanding
Leveraging Differences

Legacy
Developing Others
Managing Performance
Interpersonal Understanding
Leveraging Differences

Vision

Execute

Legacy

Great Leaders (MGL). Attending this introduction to Caterpillar's leadership framework is an expectation of every leader within the firm and is highly recommended to all frontline supervisors. In 2005, CEO Jim Owens and his team participated in the Making Great Leaders event—an introduction to the Caterpillar Leadership Framework with 360-degree assessments to help leaders become more effective. This program was designed to center the entire organization around the specific leadership competencies and styles that anchor educational programs and tie in to performance management.

The College of Leadership believes that leaders must develop new skills and abilities as they move through a successful career. Important "teachable moments" occur when a person is given a new assignment that calls for a new identity or sense of perspective. The first major opportunity for this typically occurs when a person becomes a supervisor for the first time. The COL has developed its supervisory curriculum, Succeeding in Supervision, in collaboration with DDI. The next key transition occurs when the leader must achieve results through managing others who have supervisory responsibility. Caterpillar is currently in the process of designing a program for manager development.

As individuals move on to the director or department-head level, they have the opportunity to participate in the Making Great Leaders program, and selected high-potential individuals are invited to participate in Leadership Quest. This program was designed in partnership with Duke Corporate Education and is offered twice each year to individuals nominated by succession planning to work with fifteen to twenty officers during the week-long program. The top 120 leaders in the company are also invited to an annual session called the Strategic Review Conference (SRC), in which progress in achieving strategic objectives is reviewed and challenges for the immediate future are identified. Individuals who have reached the executive level may also be invited to participate in one of the top university-based executive programs. The major educational programs to help a leader move through the stages of a successful career are shown in Figure A.5.

At Caterpillar, the CEO, divisional executives, HR staff, learning and development teams, the College of Leadership, and its advisory

Figure A.5. Core leadership programs.

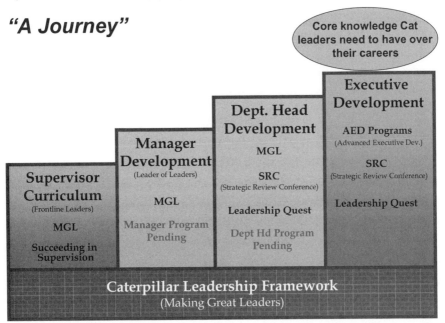

board are all involved in the design or implementation of the organization's leadership-development programs. According to college representatives, Caterpillar's top executives demonstrate sponsorship and support for leadership development. For example, CEO Jim Owens owns the "PEOPLE" critical success factor (CSF) and sits on the Caterpillar University board of governors. Owens and many on his team teach at the biannual Leadership Quest program—a week-long learning experience to help prepare high-potential leaders for future executive positions.

Caterpillar's leadership programs focus on such topics as building self-awareness, change management, diversity, ethics, financial management, globalization, innovation, integrity, interpersonal behavior skills, leadership styles, motivation/empowerment, performance management, quality, specific strategic initiatives, strategic planning, succession planning, systems thinking, values, and vision.

The college leverages a variety of approaches and tools in its leadership programs, including leaders as teachers, action learning, instructor-led classroom learning, case-based discussion, leadership and/or facilitation of one or more communities of practice, electronic performance-support systems, experiential learning, interactive TV, intranet, job assignments/rotations, mentoring/coaching, multimedia CBT, special assignments, and teleconferencing.

The College of Leadership spends approximately $5 million per year on leadership-development activities (excluding Six Sigma), and it has six full-time and three part-time employees dedicated to leadership-development activities.

While the COL emphasizes enterprise-wide initiatives to create consistency and alignment, it also promotes the concept of individualized learning. The best development must be centered on the learner; consequently, learners are encouraged to take an active role in their own development. Caterpillar emphasizes the value of lifelong learning and supports individualized needs by offering on-demand resources, coaching, e-learning, and other alternatives.

Succession Planning

The succession-planning group works closely with the COL in support of leadership development. Both groups believe that what they do must link closely to enterprise strategy. One of the big challenges currently facing Caterpillar is that it is experiencing rapidly changing demographics. As is true for many global organizations, Caterpillar's greatest growth is coming from the Asia-Pacific region, South America, and Eastern Europe. With the retirement of baby boomers already beginning and with growth outside the United States, the leadership team will be much more diverse than it is today.

Caterpillar's global succession-planning process is a robust, technology-enabled process for identifying and developing talent. It engages the entire Caterpillar leadership team to manage and optimize talent requirements over time. And it provides future leaders and technical experts with the experiences necessary to lead Caterpillar into the future. Some of the most significant aspects of the organization's succession-planning process are:

▲ It is comprehensive and includes all 36,000-plus of Caterpillar's professional employees.

▲ It is multidimensional, with inputs from individual, line management, functional, and administrative leadership.

▲ It is one common, global process supported by one system, organization-wide.

▲ It is enabled by the culture and the "yellow blood" culture (employee commitment and allegiance to Caterpillar).

Many current employees have been with the organization more than thirty years. Caterpillar's attrition rate is approximately 3 percent, much lower than the national average.

The integration of leadership-development activities is illustrated in Figure A.6. Although job experience is believed to account for 70 percent of total development, this component is considered in concert with mentoring and coaching as well as the 10 percent that comes from education and training.

Figure A.6. Integrated leadership development.

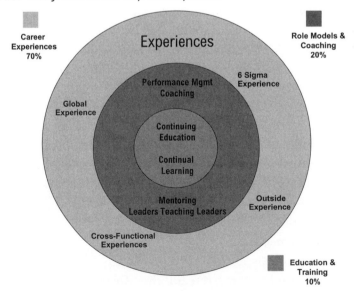

Caterpillar places great emphasis on global experiences, Six Sigma experiences, and cross-functional/cross-business assignments. Almost every person considered for officer roles will have "touched these bases."

Succession planning is a corporate function, with only four full-time employees supporting the process. They are the global process owners who work through each of the business units from a professional succession-planning standpoint to look at each one of the management employees in their organization. Functional groups (e.g., marketing, accounting, and engineering) also have succession-planning responsibilities. These succession-planning groups are responsible for the health of the functional pipeline and look across the organization to move people among business units when this would serve an important developmental purpose. This prevents key talent from becoming too siloed and ensures that talent is shared across the businesses. These are not strictly rotational job assignments. Sometimes people are transferred to gain experience and then come back to their "homes." In other instances, they remain in the new functional areas. The decision is based on the employees' interests and the enterprise's needs. Everyone is viewed as corporate talent.

Caterpillar's annual talent-identification and assessment process takes place during a four-month cycle. It focuses on the business units' leadership communicating with their leaders and employees. The employees go online and update their datasheets (internal resumes). Once an employee updates his or her datasheet, a supervisor will update the career-planning tab of the resume. The career-planning tab contains information about the employee's recommended next moves and what career experiences he or she needs. Any time it is updated, the supervisor will discuss it with the employee. Once the supervisor has had that conversation, he or she will assess the employee's longer-term potential. ("Longer-term" refers to ten years or more and the potential indicators for future promotions the employee demonstrates.) Then they hold a consensus process. For higher grades, this involves the employee's supervisor/manager, the business-unit management team, the officer team, and the executive office. For midlevel and lower grades, the consensus process involves the employee's manager, the business-unit leadership team, and the functional succession-planning groups. This group validates the employee's longer-term potential and his or her career-development plan. This process is outlined in Figure A.7.

During the detailed (career planning) discussions, supervisors and managers are encouraged to speak openly about the employee's longer-term potential without revealing the actual indicator to the employee. They do give high potentials certain indicators that should tell them they are on that track, such as having them participate in the Leadership Quest program or offering them additional incentive compensation.

Caterpillar's succession-planning group built its online career-planning tool with the help of third-party vendor Authoria. Employees fill out work history on a previous-experience tab and revise their credentials at least annually. This information is regularly reviewed, as Caterpillar strives to give employees the best developmental experiences.

Caterpillar proactively moves employees using the succession-planning move matrix. They review those employees who are ready to move, looking at their recommended next positions and career

Figure A.7. Dynamic talent identification and assessment process.

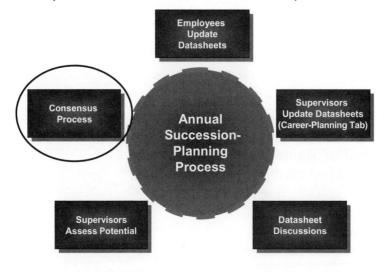

experiences, then run that against open positions to see if they find a match. Each one of the functional succession-planning groups has access to the talent-management system and uses it to generate candidate lists for openings as they occur.

A final aspect of the succession-management process is ongoing candidate selection. Although hiring managers are not told whom they should select, they are expected to seek input from HR representatives in the business unit and succession management. For lower-level management, the hiring manager posts a job and contacts local HR and functional succession-planning groups for candidate lists. Someone from HR will run a search from the succession-planning database and give the hiring manager a list of candidates who may not have seen the posting but are potentially qualified candidates. For midlevel manager positions, the appropriate functional succession-planning group provides the hiring manager with a list of candidates. The hiring manager then determines his or her short list and then presents it to the succession-planning group for its approval/support. For higher salary grades, the executive office makes the final hiring decision with input from the respective VP and global succession-management office. At this level, the vice president of the business unit requests a list of qualified candidates from global succession management, identifies a short list of three candidates, and then creates a write-up about the strategic and tactical leadership challenges the position will be expected to face over the next three to five years. This write-up goes in a binder to the executive office. The succession-planning group meets monthly with the group presidents and the CEO to review candidates and make decisions about open positions at senior levels. A key point is that one global process coordinates the development of approximately 400 key leaders.

Succession planning believes that most of Caterpillar's low- and mid-level management employees have upward mobility. Of the organization's senior management, approximately 72 percent have cross-functional experience, and approximately 75 percent have global experience.

Projects underway for enhancing the firm's succession planning include:

▲ A global diversity/inclusion strategic-improvement project

▲ A technical leaders succession-planning/career path

▲ Management of dual-career Caterpillar employees

▲ Succession planning for production employees

▲ Increased activities to employ midcareer hires

▲ Onboarding process for new and midcareer hires

Evaluating Success

The economic recession of 2001–2002 elevated Caterpillar University's need to establish the "value proposition" for organizational learning. Each college was expected to develop a value proposition for each of its key initiatives based on net benefits, ROI, and other data. The group produced a 161-page document titled "The Business of Learning," which discussed the state of learning at Caterpillar, articulated the value propositions, and estimated that the ROI for Caterpillar University exceeded 50 percent in 2003.

This effort was followed by seven detailed ROI studies that involved focus groups, surveys, in-depth discussion with participants to identify dollar benefits, cost, net benefits and improvements in productivity, quality, or reductions in cost. Chris Arvin, who was trained as an accountant, and Merrill Anderson, of MetrixGlobal, provided leadership in the methodology used in these studies.

Over time, the COL has moved from a strict assessment of ROI to an emphasis on return on learning (ROL). According to Arvin, it is important to focus on the ROL to gain a deeper understanding of how learning and development connect to business goals and objectives. Through an ROL study, the College of Leadership attempts to understand the costs and benefits, ensure benefits are greater than costs, ensure ROL percent exceeds corporate hurdle rates and compares favorably with the other investments, learn how to reduce costs and increase benefits, focus process owners and leaders on the importance of participation and application, manage the deployment for success (achieve the target ROL), take a three-stage approach to ROL (estimate ROL at development, forecast after pilot, and complete ROL at close), and use the benefit calculations to aggregate the impact of learning. Metrics in an ROL study include program costs (over a five-year period) and the opportunity cost.

The study will ask questions about benefits, amount of increases in team and personal productivity, quality improvement, and the amount sales increased. The College of Leadership will then quantify the ROL per person. This is achieved through the basic formula (gross benefits – costs)/costs. Arvin believes that it is important to establish the value proposition in each new initiative, but he suggests that it may be redundant and overly expensive to repeat this study with every iteration of a program.

The College of Leadership focuses on level 3 valuations (measuring the applicability of the learning) as well as some level 4 and 5 studies. Some of the measures and tools used for the valuations include:

▲ Participant reaction

▲ Knowledge gain

▲ Behavior change

▲ Organizational impact

▲ Return-on-investment studies

▲ 360-degree surveys

▲ Employee opinion survey

For consistency in metric evaluations, the COL believes that it is important to focus on the quality of programs delivered. For level 1 program evaluation, Caterpillar University uses learning-quality index (LQI) measures. The LQI monitors three questions: (1) Was the learning relevant to my work? (2) Will I apply the learning? (3) Will I recommend the learning to others? The COL staff monitors the LQI percentages on a monthly and year-to-date basis.

Innovative Practice

The College of Leadership achieves program excellence through the consistent use of its leaders-as-teachers concept. The concept is a key element in the following College of Leadership programs:

▲ *Leadership Quest*—a weeklong learning experience to help prepare high-potential leaders for future executive positions.

▲ *Leaders Building Leaders*—a quarterly forum in which Caterpillar leaders get to learn from the best—other Caterpillar leaders.

▲ *Values in Action*—A Code of Conduct and New Enterprise Strategy deployment, a cascade of workshops conducted globally in the fourth and first quarters of 2005–2006.

The most recent program that embraced the leaders-as-teachers concept was the enterprise deployment of the Values in Action. The program, taught by 8,000 leaders, was delivered to all employees. The cascade process was accomplished with the organization's leaders teaching the code and strategy in four phases. The initial phase consisted of the executive office teaching the top 600 leaders globally at six locations. Subsequent phases culminated by the end of January 2006 with front-line leaders teaching their employees. The outcome was the alignment of employee goals to the Values in Action strategy. Also, the leaders-as-teachers concept continues to be embedded in the organization, as business units focus on leadership initiatives and encode Six Sigma.

Lessons Learned

One key lesson learned for COL is the need to sustain the gains. In other words, success can be fleeting unless there is a constant effort to adapt and improve. Despite internal and external recognition, the College of Leadership does not rest on its laurels. After receiving program evaluations with extremely high rankings, the team immediately begins considering what can be improved for the next iteration. Accountability and changed behaviors are key objectives of all developmental activities. Other lessons learned have led to the following goals:

▲ Ensure executive sponsors.

▲ Agree on an enterprise-leadership framework and integrate it with core HR processes.

▲ Create ownership for development beyond HR to all leaders.

▲ Help leaders become teachers.

▲ Find allies for quick wins.

▲ Keep the faith and be persistent.

Cisco Systems

Site Visit Hosts:

▲ Lisa Cavallaro, Manager, WW Leadership Development

▲ Beryl Fajardo, Manager, WW Leadership Development

▲ Pat Keating, Director, WW Leadership Development

▲ Patrick Tse, Manager, WW Leadership Development

Organization Overview

Cisco Systems (Cisco) was founded in 1984 by a group of scientists from Stanford University. It is a worldwide leader in networking for the Internet with core technologies in routing and switching, and advanced technologies including VoIP, security, mobility, and video. Cisco has 48,296 employees and achieved $34.6 billion in annual revenues in its 2006 fiscal year. In 2004, the company was number two in its industry on *Fortune* magazine's "America's Most Admired Companies" list and in 2007 it was ranked number eleven on the magazine's list of the "100 Best Companies to Work For."

Over the years, Cisco's name has become synonymous with technology innovation. Additionally, the organization has a culture of giving back to the community. The organization implemented its Networking Academies in more than 160 countries, and many of the academies partner with schools and community colleges.

Cisco's mission is "Changing the way we work, live, play, and learn." According to Pat Keating, director of WW Leadership Development, change is "baked" into the way that Cisco's employees work, and that integration plays a key role in leadership at Cisco.

Before 2001, company revenue was gained primarily though growth. The company now emphasizes the balance between growth and productivity; everyone, from the CEO to the front-line manager, has a responsibility to increase productivity. Through leadership development, managers learn to be productive through growth and better processes.

When Cisco was experiencing its rapid growth, time to market was the most important metric. The company organized itself functionally in business units. Certain businesses would produce, engineer, develop/design, and market their own products under the Cisco umbrella. The functional organization had the downsides of redundancy and competition within the organization. As the company has matured, its leaders have realized the necessity of collaboration and cross-functional teamwork. Collaboration has become a major business strategy—it is included in all programs and corporate culture initiatives.

The CEO believes that executives have a deep responsibility to develop internal employees across the organization. All employees are encouraged to both "teach and take." Teams and individuals at all levels are rewarded and compensated on how well they collaborate. One of four main factors in the annual bonus plan is teamwork and collaboration.

Leadership-Development Philosophy

"Build to lead, build to last."

—John Chambers, CEO, Cisco Systems

Cisco's business strategy currently concentrates on growth and increased productivity. According to Keating, Cisco's rapid growth was abruptly halted by the dot-com collapse that occurred in the late 1990s. This financial hardship created a culture in which people continued to operate in the start-up mode, which makes them more inclined to buy talent rather than build it. Cisco realizes that to achieve its strategy, it needs to make three essential shifts.

1. The leader role must shift from achieving technical and business results to achieving excellence in leading people and developing talent through experience, exposure, and education.

2. Learning must shift from the production of education events to a holistic view of development.

3. Individual effort must be enhanced by teamwork and collaboration.

Helping people accomplish these three shifts is important in leadership education.

Today, Cisco's Worldwide (WW) Leadership Development group operates as a corporate learning unit responsible for the development of five Cisco Leadership Series programs designed to build leadership bench strength and the next generation of Cisco leaders. The vision of the group is to "build leaders to create the future." Its mission is to design and develop high-impact leadership programs that provide strong grounding in leadership foundations and accelerate major transitions, both business and personal. The WW Leadership Development group designs all programs to improve specific behaviors that are aligned with the expectations of Cisco leaders. WW Leadership Development reports to the senior vice president of human resources.

Cisco uses a leadership-review process that drives (and is driven by) three key development accelerators: (1) executive coaching, (2) the Cisco Leadership Series, and (3) the leadership fellows program. This case study focuses on the Cisco Leadership Series (Figure B.1).

Figure B.1. Cisco leadership series.

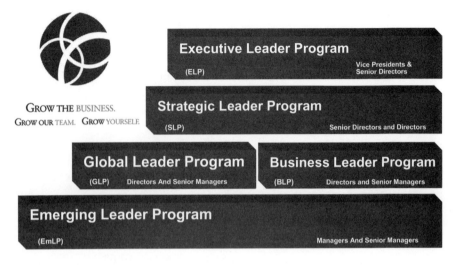

Developing Leadership Strategy

Cisco has two master frameworks for leadership development:

1. *The Grow Model.* "Grow the business; Grow our team; Grow yourself." The model includes 360-degree assessments, and all competency work is built around the model. Approximately 20 percent of the company's employees are targeted as high potential. Of those, a small percentage receive an average of twelve months of coaching performed by an external organization. The goal of the coaching is to help the leaders grow their teams.

2. *The 3E Model.* "Experience, Education, and Exposure." The model helps employees develop through on-the-job experience. Education plays a role in preparing people for the experience. Then, employees are exposed to a 360-degree view of the business and their roles in it. The Cisco Leadership Series is the education portion of that framework.

The goal of WW Leadership Development is to be recognized as number one or number 2 in corporate leadership education as measured by program innovation and business impact. Education innovation incorporates technology, design, and evaluation. According to Keating, they do not innovate for innovation's sake, but for impact.

Another goal of WW Leadership Development is to build and retain a pipeline of next-generation leadership. Its focus is transitioning from event-based, through process-based, to relationship-based—where leaders recognize the impact of education on the client and business. The target audience of WW Leadership Development is the top talent of the company. Eight thousand employees constitute the group considered to have significant growth potential and projected growth impact in the next twelve to thirty-six months. These employees are located globally and across all functions; they hold the following positions: vice president (330), director (3,000), and manager (4,600).

WW Leadership Development increases the leadership bench strength. Candidates are nominated through the leadership-review process. Because candidates for the Cisco Leadership Series are nominated, the group does not need to communicate about the program to the larger employee population. After the candidates are selected through the leadership-review process, the team works with them so they understand the applicable program.

Cisco encourages its employees to take responsibility for their own development, and so although the WW Leadership Development group does not proactively communicate and promote the Cisco Leadership Series, it does post information regarding the programs on the Web. Employees also learn about the series through observation and word of mouth. Additionally, leaders talk about their experiences in the programs, and employees see them receiving promotions.

Ties to the Business Strategy

A key to successful leadership development is business sponsorship. Each program has an executive sponsor who acts as both champion and change agent at the corporate level. The sponsors guide the program design so it fits tightly with the company's business strategy.

An example of a sponsor's role in the development of a program is the creation of the newly implemented Global Leader Program (described later in this chapter). The vice president of the Global Operations group, who holds responsibility for delivering the hardware and the field engineering support for the company worldwide, identified the need for the program. Global Operations has a staff of 250 people who work in many countries individually or in small groups. Leaders in global operations need to lead virtual teams in various environments. One of the vice president's top performers told him that, although he really wanted to take a leadership course, he needed one that would help him operate in a global environment and that the (then) current programs did not meet that need.

To make the objectives of the course a reality, the vice president presented his idea to human resources, which agreed to partner with global operations to create the solution. The impetus for developing the Global Leader Program was to help leaders think and act globally without having to send them to external training. The program's sponsor and steering committee emphasize courage, developing teams, and thinking globally as key elements of the program. The sponsor solicited expertise internally and externally. Currently, faculty from the University of California at Berkeley and the University of Singapore combine their talents with leadership mind-set experts and corporate executives to present components of the course.

Ties to Culture and Values

According to Pat Keating, director of WW Leadership Development, "programs must be grounded in what the business wants in terms of leadership development." All programs are designed to improve specific behaviors that are aligned with the expectations of Cisco leaders. Cisco's vision is to change the way the world lives, works, learns, and plays. Learning and development are integral parts of Cisco's culture. The collaboration between executive sponsors and the WW Leadership Development team epitomizes Cisco's drive to change the world. Senior executives sponsor the various programs in the Cisco Leadership Series and play active roles in program strategy and objectives as well as actual program execution.

Each program employs executive faculty, who bring strategic perspectives and access to the program. In turn, executive participation is highly valued and monitored within the organization. Measurements of participation by executives are accessible by the CEO and his direct staff via a leadership dashboard.

The Cisco Leadership Series has a strong reputation and is in high demand. All programs have a high level of participant satisfaction. Two of the programs (the Action Learning Forum and the Executive Leader Program) are catalyzing organizational changes in how senior management communicates and clarifies company strategy. They are essential to the transition from a product-based company to a solutions-based company.

The Leadership-Competency Model

Cisco has identified the Grow model (described at the beginning of this section) as the set of competencies held by its successful leaders. The "grow the business" component includes success with customers, focus on profitability and productivity, and business knowledge. The "grow our team" component involves promoting teamwork and collaboration, having vision and alignment, leading change, and building talent. The "grow yourself" component includes integrity, judgment and perspective, continuous learning, communications and influence, and adaptability. Competency also involves courage; courageous leadership is woven deeply into Cisco culture.

Budget for Leadership Development

Cisco spends $10 million a year for its formal leadership-development programs but operates on a zero-based budget. For example, for the Global Leader Program, the nominees' departments pay for their participation; the chargeback fee is $7,500 per person for the entire program.

Departments cover the participants' salaries during their time in the residential portion of the program. Each department at Cisco has funding for development and travel. The fact that departments are willing to invest in leadership training for their best employees is a sign that the training is successful, according to WW Leadership representatives.

Building an Integrated Leadership Roadmap

Program-manager and program-coordinator teams design and run each program—they are held accountable for not only the design and results but also the costs. WW Leadership Development works closely with business partners to design the programs, and it is responsible for delivering them.

Program managers also act as business managers. According to Keating, these managers need four skills: (1) strong program-management capabilities so they can orchestrate, design, and deliver complex programs; (2) instructional design expertise; (3) the ability to use technology to deliver learning; and (4) business acumen. The program managers ensure that all training is related to the business. Recent hires have been from the business segment rather than from the HR segment; Keating strives for a mix of talent.

Alignment

Alignment of Cisco's leadership-development programs and business strategy occurs through the executive committees. WW Leadership Development aligns with a broader talent-management process through the 3E model described in the previous section. The basic leadership model involves a 360-degree process at the functional level; each functional lead has a talent review with the head of HR, who owns the talent-management process. As the functions go through the process and review top talent with HR, their decisions flow up to the board.

Cisco currently does not have formal succession planning. Vice presidents in business units work with HR to review their own top talent and critical positions.

Leadership-Development Approaches and Tools

The programs that make up the Cisco Leadership Series operate in a three-phase structure that facilitates the employee's ability to put learning into action. This is an "events to process" model. Employees involved in the various programs progress through each phase.

Phase 1—the participants go through preparation, diagnosis of their current level, reflection, and virtual projects with other program participants in their cohort. Through self-directed learning and conversations with their managers, learners become clear on their objectives for going through the program and come prepared to participate fully.

Phase 2—the participants reside at a conference center or meeting place and participate in workshops, networking events, and activities. This is the traditional learning event.

Phase 3—the participants return to their jobs to apply the results. The previous two phases drive to application; all program design is focused on behavior gain and business impact. The design team knows what behavior it expects to drive when it designs the programs, and it tracks the impact of the program.

The Cisco Leadership Series consists of five programs, all built at different times.

1. The Emerging Leader Program is foundational and serves experienced managers with approximately three years on the job; it covers personal and team leadership. Approximately 500 employees are selected for the program each year. Its executive sponsor is the vice president, corporate finance.

2. The Business Leader Program focuses on directors and senior managers. The company considers it "an MBA in a box," getting into the foundations of finance, strategy, and leadership. It teaches core business skills and is presented to approximately 400 people a year. Its executive sponsor is the senior vice president of corporate development.

3. The Global Leader Program was implemented in 2005. Like the Business Leader Program, it focuses on directors and senior managers

and teaches personal leadership and business fundamentals. However, it concentrates on employees whose responsibilities include managing teams in multiple countries. It serves approximately 200 people annually, and the workshop takes place around the world: Singapore, Athens, Barcelona, etc. Management has made an executive decision not to deliver the program in its San Jose headquarters because the travel allows participants and presenters to achieve a global mind-set. Its executive sponsor is the vice president of technical support.

4. The Action Learning Forum is built on the Business Leader Program and focuses on senior directors and directors responsible for accelerating the fulfillment of the company's plans and building its capabilities. Annually, 92 employees are involved in the program. In partnership with its research and development group focused on emerging technologies, participants in the program take actual emerging technologies and determine their place in Cisco's development strategy. At the end of the program, action learning teams make recommendations to the technology board on the direction the company should pursue in relation to the emerging technology. The company is transitioning from being product-based to being systems-and-solutions-based, and the program will prepare leaders for this change. Its executive sponsor is the vice president of marketing.

5. The Executive Leader Program focuses on the company's strategic intent and serves approximately forty top leaders annually. The Executive Leader Program was designed for employees who are newly promoted to the vice-presidential level or who are filling a vice-presidential role. (Currently, the number of vice presidents in the organization is approximately 200.) Its executive sponsor is the senior vice president of operations.

On the following pages, the Global Leader and Emerging Leader programs are described in depth.

Global Leader Program

The Global Leader Program began early in 2005 and has served 240 people in six sessions. Its success is attributable, in part, to the strong executive sponsorship of the program. Human resources, global operations, and outside consultants designed the course based on input and feedback from individuals who had completed the Executive Leader Program. The executive leadership group that provided the initial input became the program's executive steering committee.

After the program was implemented, the steering committee adjusted it based on feedback from participants in the first session. The feedback included suggestions regarding how to make the content more relevant to Cisco (both culturally and from the business perspective). The steering committee, which met monthly at first, now meets quarterly to review course objectives and future direction.

The core program is delivered by a program manager and coordinator. The content is developed with input from HR, subject-matter experts, and external consultants. The delivery team receives additional input from the steering committee to ensure relevance to the business. When applicable, the steering committee invites vice presidents to sit in on the program. It also asks a vice president to kick the program off, a task that not only demonstrates top leadership support but also gives the vice presidents an opportunity to share their experiences and challenges with the participants.

Designers of the Global Leader Program have created an impact map that summarizes business impact, job results, behavior changes, and required knowledge and actions (Figure B.2). The impact map states that the program is for senior managers and directors with global responsibilities or direct reports who do not reside in their countries. The impact map designates that participation in the program is by nomination only. A typical session involves forty participants, and they are selected across various functions and business focuses.

The impact map states that the three key job results for the program are (1) a global leader mind-set, (2) a global strategy, and (3) global teaming ability. The program introduces a concept, demonstrates it, allows participants to practice it, and solicits feedback from the participant. All programmatic activity is designed to lead to a changed mind-set.

The Global Leader Program lasts twenty weeks and uses the three-

Figure B.2. Global Leader Program impact map.

Prerequisites	Program Objective: to further develop the global mind-set and skill set of Cisco's global management team			
• Senior Managers and Directors (Grades 12, 13, or equivalent. Grade 11 with significant growth potential)	Know and Do	Behaviors	Job Results	Business Impact
	What are the essential Mind-sets, Skill-sets Tool sets that the program delivers?	What will participants do differently as a result of participation in CLS?	What important job results will usage of the program achieve or improve?	Toward what business goals do these job results primarily contribute?
• Global Responsibilities				
Selection & Logistics	• Translate Cisco's global priorities into organizational goals	• Demonstrate the behaviors and mind-sets required for successful global leadership	• Increased focus on global mind-set as demonstrated by my actions and interactions	• Customer Satisfaction
• By Nomination Only selection determined by your business group's senior leadership team and Leadership Education	• Drive innovative global business practices by leveraging local competencies and culture and global relationships and networks	• Apply the principles of global strategy at Cisco		• Growth
		• Leverage your own cultural intelligence to inspire and lead global teams	• An active role in driving global strategy	• Market Share
• Global Participation & Cross-Functional Representation		• Apply the critical elements of global teaming to increase team performance	• Improved team communications and increased team productivity	• Profitability
• Program delivered outside of San Jose	• Inspire others to act as global leaders	• Build and strengthen your informal global network		
• Cost: $7,500 Participant (Excludes T&E)	• Build a culture of trust and mutual accountability		• Improved collaboration with others outside my country	
• Cohort Size: 40	• Create high-performance global teams by enrolling people in a shared and aspirational purpose			

phase structure. Phase 1 includes prereadings, an assessment for development, an initial coaching call on the initiative, manager discussions, and the introduction of a development tracker. Each participant comes into the program with an initiative, and the facilitators help the participants work their way through the initiatives, which are tracked on the development tracker, and participants receive executive mentoring on their projects. Phase 2 is a four-and-a-half-day residential workshop that focuses on translating Cisco's global priorities into organizational goals, driving innovative global business practices, inspiring others to act as global leaders, building a culture of trust and mutual accountability, and creating high-performance global teams. Phase 3 takes twelve weeks and contains a coaching session, three learning-pod sessions, and a virtual session with Cisco executives (typically sponsors of the program). Learning pods are small groups created during the residential session and facilitated by an executive coach. In the pods, the participants are able to discuss some of the challenges they are facing as they return to the workplace to forward their initiative. During the virtual session with Cisco executives, the executives learn ways to improve the program.

Figure B.3 is a sample agenda for Phase 2 of a Global Leader Program session. A typical agenda begins with a presentation made by an executive leader, often the program sponsor or member of the steering committee. He or she speaks about personal experiences and obstacles overcome. On the second day, the participants learn about global strategy, including competitive intelligence, markets, and organizing for global effectiveness. On the third day, participants learn cultural intelligence and how to build effective global teams. The week ends with an inspirational call to action and a dialogue with executives. Participants have an opportunity to chat with executives in an informal environment. Formal demand on an executive is typically six hours in a twenty-week period.

WW Leadership Development delivered six Global Leader sessions and served 202 participants in fiscal year 2006. Plans for 2007 included action-learning pods, more coaching, a bonus session following each program offering for program alumni, and other alumni events. Currently, the residential portion of the Global Leader Program is four days, but it could be expanded to a fifth day in which program alumni are brought back to mentor, share success stories, and listen to thought-leader speakers.

WW Leadership Development sees forty participants as ideal for

Figure B.3. GLP Phase 2 agenda.

	Sunday	Monday	Tuesday	Wednesday	Thursday	Friday

A M		8:30 am
		Opening & Welcome
		MIND-SET OF A
		GLOBAL LEADER
		- Framing
		- Cisco Executive
		  Sponsor
			8:30 am
			Opening & Framing
			GLOBAL
			STRATEGY
			- Sources of
			  Competitive
			  Advantage
			  Globally
				8:30 am
				Opening & Framing
				CULTURAL
				INTELLIGENCE
					8:30 am
					Opening & Framing
					INSPIRING ACTION
					IN SELF AND
					OTHERS
					- Cisco Executive
					  Dialogue	

P M		MINDSET OF A
		GLOBAL LEADER
		- The Courageous
		  Leader
		- Global
		  Awareness
		- Responsible
		  Mind-set
			GLOBAL
			STRATEGY
			- Understanding
			  the Drivers of
			  Market Structure
			- Organizing for
			  Global
			  Effectiveness
				GLOBAL TEAMING
				- Building
				  Effective Global
				  Teams
				- Leading Teams
				  in Complex
				  Environments
					Application
					Commitments
					- Prep for Phase 3
					- Evaluation and
					  Close (3:30 pm)	

E V E	6:30 pm Session begins Welcome Reception Dinner	Dinner	Group Dinner - Off-site	Dinner with your Learning Pod		

the program, allowing for comfortable facilitation by two individuals and the opportunity to break the group up into six learning pods with approximately six to seven individuals in each pod. As few as thirty people have composed a session, but demand for the program is growing, and future classes should support the forty-participant limit.

Participants discuss content area, perform exercises, and receive feedback in the cross-functional, cross-theater learning pods. At the end of each day, participants gather in the pods to discuss how to integrate what they learned with the initiative that they have brought into the program. Cisco uses the learning-pod model to enable networking after the participants return to work. Program managers and coordinators facilitate each pod.

Emerging Leader Program

The Emerging Leader Program is a thirteen-week integrated experience designed to develop and build Cisco's bench strength. Participants in the program must be working at the manager level and identified as high-potential candidates. During a portion of the program, participants are taken out of their day-to-day management activities; they learn about strategy, financial decisions, and how to communicate strategy to the rest of the organization. In part, the focus of the program is helping employees transition from manager to leader, helping them make wise decisions regarding their priorities.

As with the Global Leader Program, the Emerging Leader Program has an executive committee with seven members; the committee has cross-business and cross-geographic representation. Sometimes the reality of day-to-day management interferes with the vision necessary to be a leader, but executives and facilitators work with the participants to establish a balance between the two. Participants' managers play a critical role in supporting the participants throughout the program and especially in Phase 3 as they pursue applying what they learn back on the job. Three aspects of the program help the participant use what he or she has learned in the workplace: relevance of program, visibility, and accountability. Employees who succeed are accountable for their results and visible in their ability to demonstrate what they have done. Employees should be able to tie what they have learned directly to their annual employee reviews.

When the Emerging Leader Program was developed, it consisted of a two-week, event-based course delivery and a subsequent evaluation, which was considered the finish line for learning. The program has since transitioned to the three-phase structure common to all programs in the Cisco Leadership Series; it is a thirteen-week blended learning program. The finish line now occurs after a period of transfer and application of knowledge. Participants reach the finish line when they demonstrate workplace performance results such as growth and increased market share.

Participants and their managers are much more satisfied with the redesigned program. Advantages include innovative blended modalities, a focus on interactions rather than transactions, management and executive engagement, professional coaching through all phases, assessments and insight, development and impact trackers that record experiences throughout the program, and essential-shifts assessment.

The assessment of the Emerging Leader Program is built around the three essential shifts described in the first section of this case study. A preassessment is conducted in week one of phase one of the program and is repeated in week eleven of the program. Results of the assessment demonstrate that participants progress significantly across all shifts, and the pattern of shifts continues through postassessment. Participants show the greatest change in shifting from success in achieving technical and business results to excellence in leading people and developing talent through experience, exposure, and education.

Approximately 85 percent of learning in the Emerging Leader Program is done with small-group interaction and collaboration. Phase 1 involves six weeks of self-directed learning supported by faculty, executives, and a program office. The program begins with a virtual kickoff meeting and assessments for development. Each participant receives three hours of individualized consultation by a certified coach. In week four, the participants form cohorts, which are virtual simulation teams comprising approximately twenty-five cross-functional individuals involved in community building. Each cohort is sponsored by at least two executives, who remain with it throughout the session. The executives share experiences, stories, and challenges with the participants. Participant time commitment for phase one is two hours per week.

Phase two involves role play, leadership simulation, peer feedback, executive sponsorship, coaching, and community building conducted in a one-week workshop called an onsite leadership-learning lab. The term *lab* is used to communicate that the participants are experiencing more than traditional training. Experimentation, risk-taking, and discussion are encouraged.

The cohort has five simulation teams comprising four or five people. The simulation team leads a fictitious company through three quarters of a fiscal year. Through the process, participants experience various leadership levels. Executives present to the group during phase two.

Phase three involves applying new skills on the job, community building, and reporting results and lessons learned cofacilitated by executive sponsors. Participants have formal discussions with their own managers about what they have learned.

Throughout the program, participants use a development and impact tracker to chart their progress. If they are not able to stay current in their program work, WW Leadership Development speaks with its managers to clarify that they are being allowed time to participate in the program. Very few individuals disengage from the program, which has a backlog of prospective participants eager to be a part of it.

Executive Support for Leadership Development

Members of Cisco's executive leadership team play critical roles in the organization's leadership-development programs. The roles include executive program sponsorship, executive faculty participation, vision and guidance via the executive steering committees, and sponsorship visibility at the CEO level.

High Potentials

Cisco identifies high-potential employees by using a nine-box grid. Along one axis are three levels of potential and on the other are three levels of performance. (The word *potential* is similar to *promotability*.) Decisions are made by the vice president of the business unit; there are no formal corporation-wide criteria.

Implementing the Successful Leadership-Development Strategy

As described in the following section of the case study, the WW Leadership Development group relies on feedback from participants to ensure that the content of the programs is relevant. Results of qualitative and quantitative assessments are shared with steering committees so that they can make changes to program design in collaboration with the group. The process involves visiting Cisco's business objectives and ensuring alignment between leadership-development programs and the business strategy.

Additionally, the WW Leadership Development team also uses Robert Brinkerhoff's Success Case Method (described in more detail in the "Evaluating Success" section) on a biannual basis to analyze the highlights and lowlights of the programs through both quantitative and qualitative measures. They use the results to ensure programs are relevant and use current, up-to-date content.

Implementation and Governance

As described previously, Cisco's WW Leadership Development group is primarily responsible for the implementation of the programs in the Cisco Leadership Series. The group receives support from, and leverages, executive sponsors to help deliver parts of the different programs. The group partners with clients (executives) in business units to meet the needs of the businesses. In partnership with the business units, the team designs and develops high-impact leadership programs, which build strong leadership foundations that accelerate major business and personal transitions.

Each program has an established cross-functional steering committee that strengthens the link between the program and the business. The business leaders on the steering committees help drive the design of the programs and recruit appropriate executives into the classrooms. During the design phase of the program, the steering committees meet often. The programs employ executive faculty who bring participants a strategic perspective.

Executive participation in the programs is highly valued and monitored in the company. The CEO and his direct reports can access participant information through a leadership dashboard. WW Leadership Development has one director, five program managers, and three program coordinators. Annually, it spends $10 million (U.S.) on formal leadership-development programs. The director reports to the vice president of talent development.

Evaluating Success

WW Leadership Development uses a formal system for measuring the outcomes of its leadership-development strategy. Leadership evaluation and measurement focus on the value of the investment. The company collects both quantitative and qualitative measures. Examples of metrics include price range for a one-week course, customer satisfaction scores, percentage of class graduates who have used what they have learned in their jobs and had a positive impact, and percentage of learners who stay with the company. Management celebrates cases in which satisfaction is high and costs are down; however, it realizes that participants could be satisfied, but the courses could have no business impact. The team concentrates on metrics showing the application of learning to jobs and changes in business results. The percentage of employee retention for those going through the programs compared to the general employee population is favorable—approximately 93 percent across the organization.

For the past two years, WW Leadership Development has used the Robert Brinkerhoff Success Case Method to measure the impact of its various programs. The group chose the method because it is simple, elegant, and easy to implement. The method uses case examples and success stories to describe the best (and worst) that the training is providing; it identifies what the training is doing and what it is not doing. Results are also shared with HR and sent up the management chain so they can see the value that is provided by the programs and pursue external awards.

The method begins with the creation of an impact map (see Figure B.2 for an example) that is designed to show what the organization needs to improve through leadership training: customer satisfaction, growth, market share, and profitability. The map has four columns: Key Content, Key Behaviors, Results, and Impact. According to Lisa Cavallaro, manager of leadership development, "Results are what we back into from impacts. We ask ourselves, 'To get [a stated level] of impact, what do we have to do relative to the programs we are working with?' We think strategically about how the program will drive the behaviors to achieve the impact."

All programs are designed to shift employees' mind-sets because only a transformed mind-set is likely to lead to changes in behavior. Behavioral shifts have three aspects: (1) shifting mind-sets regarding the leader's role in shaping and executing strategy, (2) providing tool sets to enable skillful application, and (3) building skill sets to meet critical strategy-execution challenges. Shifting mind-sets means re-framing leaders' roles.

For the Emerging Leader Program, the team assesses the results of its programs using a simple survey of five to eight behavior-based questions that were developed in consultation with the Brinkerhoff team. The survey is administered both before the training and six to nine months after the training ends.

WW Leadership Development surveyed 173 out of 298 participants, with 133 completing the survey for a 77 percent response rate. Ninety-eight percent of the respondents say the program had a "deliverable, measurable, concrete business impact." Results are corroborated with interviews with the participants' managers. Results include:

▲ Improved collaboration relative to customer needs (57 percent)

▲ Improved team morale and productivity (57 percent)

▲ Increased time spent developing teams (61 percent)

▲ Increased focus on implementing team initiatives and goals (67 percent)

According to Cavallaro, all results must be able to "stand up in court." If participants report that they received no deliverable, measurable business results, the team determines why they have not. Negative results are used by the design team to improve the learning and development product.

Results show that leadership-development programs have a direct impact on two aspects of a manager's role: performance management and collaboration. Leadership development improves performance management by giving managers the tools and skills they need to:

▲ Handle critical performance issues

▲ Bring new members of the team aboard and make them highly productive

▲ Identify poor performers and counsel them out of Cisco

▲ Apply effective performance-management principles

▲ Improve the relationship between themselves and their direct reports

Teamwork and collaboration are essential in Cisco's culture. The networking that occurs in the leadership programs would not happen in any other setting. During the workshop phase of the programs, participants gain insight from listening to their peers, and a natural, healthy competition occurs when leaders assemble. According to the vice president of global operations:

Phase 2 gives employees a chance to partner with folks who are outside their silo. Now, all technical product providers are dealing with a hazardous materials legislation that requires organizations

to eliminate five different chemicals from production. This problem of how to eliminate the chemicals from the process is felt in
every business unit, and it is the perfect example of a problem that
can be talked through at cross-functional leadership development.
It is a problem that affects both manufacturing and service.

Participants stay in touch with each other and ask each other for advice on various issues; they compete in their own roles to demonstrate the value of what they have learned.

Leadership development improves teamwork and collaboration
by giving managers the tools and skills they need to:

▲ Increase collaboration across functions that had not successfully collaborated in the past

▲ Raise appreciation for the expertise and contributions of other
functional staff

▲ Improve the use of different perspectives to arrive at better
sales solutions

▲ Increase their ability to accomplish important goals while
working with others

To determine the enablers of program success, WW Leadership
Development administered a survey to the entire population of employees who had taken leadership-development programs. It identified and sampled the tail ends of the bell curve—the participants who
were exceptionally successful and the ones who were not able to put
what they learned into action. The team identified three key enablers
of program success:

1. *Nomination.* Through the nomination process, individuals
learn why they were selected; they have a clear idea of why they are
being trained and what is expected of them when they return to the
job.

2. *Learnings That Are Immediately Applicable.* Participants who

were able to put their new skills and capabilities to work immediately were most successful.

3. *Total Commitment.* Participants were engaged throughout the process, from before the workshops to after they end. They experienced a high level of interaction with managers, sponsors, and fellow participants.

These enablers were absent from surveyed participants who reported low impact.

Communicating Success

The results for the 2005 and 2006 Cisco Leadership Series are in. Participants told WW Leadership Development how they were helped by the programs. Graduates said that the networking opportunities were invaluable. They also recounted specific cases regarding how they were helped. The following examples of the impact on participants from each of the four programs in place during 2005 and 2006 are typical.

1. *Executive Leader Program.* One participant learned from program participation that engaging his team early and more strategically, with greater collaboration, can pay off. The actions he took led to faster product development and reduction in false starts, contributing to savings of approximately $1 million. Specifically, he benefited by (1) understanding his ecosystem better, (2) engaging earlier in processes with other parts of the organization, and (3) learning about core versus context and developing relationships.

2. *Action Learning Forum.* A technical-assistance program leader gained an increased understanding of the why and how of process improvement and how to link department goals to unit goals. As a result, he encouraged his team to improve the success rate of fixing software bugs, thereby reducing customer frustrations. The team then achieved a cost savings of $600,000 per year and developed a sustained capacity for working more effectively. The participant says that

he did not have the methodology to achieve these accomplishments prior to the program.

3. *Business Leader Program.* One participant was motivated and committed by the program to review strategy with her team. The team created a new product strategy that takes start-to-finish responsibility for developing security products that will lead to more than $12 million in new sales. Other new products are underway, and the team has developed a sustained change in the way it leverages collaboration and networks in its ongoing work. In the past, the team operated reactively, fighting fires. When the participant was asked whether she would have achieved so much without the program, she said that she would probably have come to the same mind-set eventually, but the program accelerated the process.

4. *Emerging Leader Program.* One participant was motivated by program participation to take dramatic new collaborative actions leading to a $50 million sale and open a new market area with promising opportunities. The program was a catalyst to leverage new opportunities and establish new relationships in his fourteen-state region.

Evaluations completed by participants consistently highlight the value of the collaboration facilitated by the programs. Because Cisco is a functional organization, participants find the development of cross-functional relationships invaluable.

Assessing for the Future

WW Leadership Development is in the process of changing its Strategic Leader Program. This program focuses on directors, senior directors, and their ability to develop strategy-execution capabilities. The Strategic Leader Program steering committee is a multidisciplinary team that is tasked with preparing individuals to be a part of the transition of the organization to a systems-and-solutions company. The key to the transition is the ability to act as an increasingly integrated organization.

The new program will be approximately six to eight weeks, be action-oriented, and operate in partnership with Cisco's new Emerging Technologies group. Cisco sees the need to innovate, and Emerging Technologies and the talent involved in the Strategic Leader Program can work together to vet and evaluate a business case for the new ideas. If the business opportunities are implemented, the participants in the Strategic Leader Program will have the opportunity to be part of the management team driving the new business. After the new businesses are funded, Strategic Leader participants will play a role in determining marketing strategy and product launch. Finally, for new businesses that are extremely successful, participants in the program will help create a business platform to support them.

According to Keating, the transformed Strategic Leader Program "will put the experience E into the education E in a big way." WW Leadership Development is targeting four projects per quarter, with six- to eight-member teams working on a project. The challenge will be to ensure that the focus remains on development and not on team deliverables. Each team will have a vice president sponsor in addition to the program's executive sponsors for the program. Because each team will be working on a different project, WW Leadership Development sees no competition at this point. The teams will receive data support from the analysts who work in the business units with whom Emerging Technologies is working.

Innovative Aspects

Among the WW Leadership Development group's innovative practices are:

▲ Leveraging Web-based technology to develop and deliver leading-edge, blended-leadership offerings

▲ Leading the integration of Cisco's Leadership Series programs with other elements of leadership development consistent with Cisco's 3E (Experience, Education, Exposure) model of development

▲ Using Robert Brinkerhoff's Success Case Method model to

measure behavioral change and quantitative and qualitative program impact

Critical Success Factors and Lessons Learned

One key lesson learned for Cisco and the WW Leadership Development group is the need to ensure that the expertise of external (non-Cisco) speakers is applicable to the cultural and knowledge requirements of a Cisco employee. Initially, this was a real problem in some of the leadership programs. The company is complex, and often outside presenters do not understand how the company is organized. Real-world examples from other firms often fall flat. Now, the programs' executive steering committees are responsible for helping the outside presenters understand the company. Keys to the success of this (or any program) are executive support and a focus on real business problems.

PepsiCo Inc.

Site Visit Hosts:

▲ Allan H. Church, Vice President, Organization & Management Development

▲ Paul Russell, Vice President, Executive Learning & Development

Organization Overview

PepsiCo Inc. (PepsiCo) is a world leader in convenient foods and beverages, with more than 167,000 employees and 2006 revenues of more than $35 billion. PepsiCo brands are available in nearly 200 countries and territories. In addition to the corporate entity, which consists of several shared services functions (e.g., finance, legal, IT), the organization features two operating divisions: (1) PepsiCo North America, which includes Frito-Lay North America; PepsiCola North America; and Quaker, Tropicana, Gatorade North America; and (2) PepsiCo International.

Although many of PepsiCo's brand names have been around for more than a century, the organization itself is fairly young, having been founded in 1965 with the merger of Pepsi-Cola and Frito-Lay. PepsiCo acquired Tropicana in 1998 and merged with The Quaker Oats Company, including Gatorade, in 2001. PepsiCo's mission is:

> To be the world's premier consumer products company focused on convenient foods and beverages. We seek to produce healthy financial rewards to investors as we provide opportunities for growth and enrichment to our employees, our business partners and the communities in which we operate. And in everything we do, we strive for honesty, fairness and integrity.

PepsiCo believes that there are three major sustainable advantages that give the organization a competitive edge as it operates in the global marketplace: big, muscular brands; proven ability to innovate and create differentiated products; and powerful go-to-market systems. As Figure C.1 illustrates, the common denominator for these advantages is PepsiCo's own people. By taking these competitive advantages and investing in them with dollars generated from top-line

Figure C.1. PepsiCo's sustainable advantages.

growth and cost-savings initiatives, PepsiCo sustains a value cycle for its shareholders.

Developing Leadership Strategy

PepsiCo's executives strongly believe in the importance of developing the organization's current and future leaders in order to build and sustain leadership capability across the organization. Driving this belief are external demands, organizational and operational complexities, and demands on and by the organization's talent base. External demands on PepsiCo are up and not expected to decline any time soon. For example, PepsiCo has a results-oriented culture. The organization's corporate growth algorithm requires volume/revenue growth in the mid–single digits and division operating profit at approximately 8 percent. And there are unrelenting demands from Wall Street for consistently outstanding financial performance. These short-term demands require constant vigilance to ensure they don't draw attention away from the organization's longer-term talent-development needs. Additionally, PepsiCo's customer and consumer landscapes change rapidly.

In addition to those external demands, organizational and operational complexities require a leadership-development strategy that will build capabilities for the organization's future. The structure and organization required to foster growth goals are leading to progressively more complex working arrangements, such as matrixed structures. Business-process transformation is radically changing the way PepsiCo links its business, people, and information, requiring closer, tighter linkages than ever before.

Demands on and by the organization's own talent base are increasing as well. This feeds into the need to build that leadership capability. Executives and employees at all levels are challenged to work more productively, innovatively, collaboratively, inclusively, and with greater focus on the organization's values. Today's employees expect and demand developmental opportunities to stay ahead and reach their career goals. The shelf-life of an MBA education grows ever shorter, and participants value opportunities to learn new skills and tools and how to apply them within the context and culture of PepsiCo. Finally, PepsiCo's own demographics show that a significant percentage of its senior executives will be eligible for retirement in the next several years.

With all of these drivers, human resources (HR) plays a critical role. HR has a special accountability entrusted to it to nurture and develop the investment the organization makes in talent and ensure the organization's human assets are optimized. HR's challenge is to continue to build organizational capability around identifying Pep-siCo's future leaders, retaining them, and developing their experiences and mind-sets to take on and succeed in roles as general managers and functional leaders.

However, PepsiCo's HR group is not starting from scratch with its talent pool. The organization has made several improvements to the talent-development infrastructure since 2001, including:

▲ Updating the leadership-competency model and 360-degree feedback process

▲ Creating global functional (e.g., marketing, sales, finance, and HR) competency models

▲ Creating a corporate core of general, functional, and "specific audience" leadership programs

▲ Crystallizing its career-growth model

▲ Making progress in planning and using experiences more strategically

▲ Developing orientation/coaching/mentoring programs in every division

▲ Clarifying how it looks at the development process (i.e., identify, develop, move)

PepsiCo does not have a singular head to oversee all talent development. The organization is set up in a divisional structure, and each division has its own organization-development-and-training group that is responsible for the training, design, and delivery in that division. At the time of our site visit, Paul Russell was the corporate vice president of executive learning; he oversaw the core leadership curriculum across all divisions. Another individual in corporate, Allan Church (vice president of organization and management development), oversees the core HR-related processes that cross all divisions (including the talent-management process).

HR's mission and vision is to make PepsiCo a place where people want to work and to ensure the company enables talented people to make that happen. The organization requires strong leaders to succeed in the marketplace. This leadership capability increases in importance in more senior roles. To attract and retain the best people, PepsiCo needs leaders who can take others with them. Doing this requires systems and processes, insights (about the business and people), talent management, work and organization design (HR generalists are empowered and can design their organizations the way they need them to work), and culture and values. These are HR's strategic planks.

PepsiCo's HR organization uses a two-pronged approach to building talent. The first is the PepsiCo Career Growth Model (described in the next section), which provides tools, processes, and training to drive a broad-based development culture. The second prong is its talent-management model (described beginning on page 191), which provides talent segmentation and aggressive bench building to deliver growth. The key supporting principles underlying this two-pronged approach are: (1) all employees should have access to development; (2) differentiation regarding how PepsiCo manages talent is critical to the business; and (3) a focus on triangulation (data should be treated as a source of input). The HR organization grounds the approach and principles in the following insights:

- ▲ External labor trends and shifting workforce needs

- ▲ Internal opportunities, movement, and bench strength

- ▲ Attitudes, perceptions, and expectations of employees

- ▲ Skills, capabilities, experiences, and potential of talent

PepsiCo's Career Growth Model

PepsiCo's view of career growth is that it is a partnership among the employees, managers, and the organization. Employees and managers may be responsible for their own development, but the organization also has a responsibility to ensure that they are provided with opportunities to develop and grow. PepsiCo's Career Growth Model serves as the organization's core integrating tool and considers five factors: proven results, leadership capability, functional excellence, knowing the business cold, and critical experiences. (Each of the five factors is described next.) When combined together, these five factors result in opportunities and long-term career growth and success.

The model is linked to and supported by PepsiCo's people processes (e.g., performance and development reviews, 360-degree feedback, organizational and individual talent reviews, organizational-health survey, and succession planning). The model ensures a common language regarding career growth and development and alignment in all new tools. Like the leadership-development strategy, the Career Growth Model is well aligned with larger business priorities. For instance, the performance-management process starts immediately after the annual operating plan review in November each year.

Proven Results

PepsiCo requires that its employees demonstrate consistent and proven business and people results in order to be considered for future growth opportunities. They look for a track record of sustained successes as well as results that create a lasting impact. People results are also important and are a significant part of performance expectations. Managers are expected to attract, develop, and retain talent. How results are achieved is important to PepsiCo. The importance of this is driven by the organization's people processes. The performance-management process determines managers' compensation. Previously, business results accounted for 66 percent and people results for 34 percent of an individual's compensation. In 2007, that ratio changed to an even 50/50 split.

Leadership Capability

The demand for strong leaders in one of the major reasons the company has recently reviewed and enhanced its leadership model. Leadership competencies form the basis for the 360-degree feedback process and provide a reference point for measuring people results. More important, however, they also provide a framework to determine an executive's contributions to the organization as a leader over time.

When coaching an executive on his or her leadership skills/capabilities, PepsiCo considers such elements as:

▲ Consistent demonstration of particular leadership competencies

▲ Growth of leadership effectiveness over time

▲ Increasing impact (by the individual) on the organization over time

▲ Creating an inclusive work environment

▲ Development of his/her own people

▲ Amount of turnover (in this person's group)

▲ Capacity and skills to take on a more significant leadership position

PepsiCo also leverages functional competency models to help leaders develop expertise in their individual roles. Functional experience is one of the four key components of the organization's career growth model described earlier. For more on this, see the section titled "The Leadership-Competency Model."

Functional Excellence

Functional excellence is an important part of career growth at PepsiCo. PepsiCo expects its employees and managers to commit to developing their functional expertise. They need to develop an in-depth understanding of their own functions as well as learn how the various functions fit together. Some divisions use functional competency models (e.g., in marketing, sales, finance, R&D, and HR) to help their managers and people in their development, and others rely more on experiential learning experiences. After an individual demonstrates functional excellence, the basis of his or her development shifts to other areas like leader capability or critical experiences.

Knowing the Business Cold

Another element in PepsiCo's Career Growth Model, "knowing the business cold," requires that managers develop a broader knowledge of the different factors that drive growth, seek out new opportunities and experiences to enhance their understanding of the organization's markets and better enable them to "connect the dots," and take all of this and use it to make better business decisions. Good decisions are based on good business data, such as how the organization makes, sells, and delivers its products as well as understanding how and why customers, competitors, and suppliers work the way they do. The importance of knowing the business increases in importance as individuals move up the organization.

Critical Experiences

The next component of the organization's Career Growth Model is "critical experiences." Discussions of potential career moves at PepsiCo include an assessment of critical experiences (those that the individual already has, those that he or she could benefit from, and those that are needed in a potential role). Focusing on experiences provides a richer forum for discussions than focusing on positions or titles. Depth and breadth of experience become more important in more senior roles.

PepsiCo has identified a number of critical experiences to help its leaders become more well-rounded in their skills and capabilities. These eighteen experiences fall into three broad categories:

1. Experiences that come from dealing with various business challenges

2. Experiences in different roles, functions, and divisions that help develop a broader business perspective

3. Experiences and challenges that can come at any time and result in personal growth

PepsiCo does not expect its people to have all of these experiences; it uses them as a framework to understand what individuals have done so that they can leverage their current capabilities and plan for new experiences in future assignments.

A key component of this part of the model is an emphasis on building relationships with others throughout the organization (e.g., functionally, cross-functionally, and cross-divisionally). Sharing experiences with others increases an individual's in-depth knowledge of the organization, benefiting him or her across all aspects of the Career Growth Model.

Opportunities

If PepsiCo's employees are responsible for their own development, the organization is responsible for providing them with opportunities for development and growth. Managers are held accountable for the development of their people. PepsiCo provides the following guidelines for individuals and managers when considering potential opportunities.

▲ Think about experiences that would stretch you the most.

▲ Be flexible—flexibility and an open mind will provide you with a broader range of opportunities.

▲ Be patient—don't impose unrealistic expectations on titles or timing.

▲ Remember that a career is a long-term journey—look for opportunities consistent with your career goals; don't move for the sake of moving.

▲ Build for the long term—lateral moves can be as richly developing as moves to higher levels.

PepsiCo identifies individuals as high potentials during its People Planning process. Below are answers to questions commonly asked by employees regarding this process:

▲ *How do I get on a slate?* In addition to demonstrating functional expertise, an employee must also show a breadth of capabilities and experiences. Leadership skills take a high degree of importance in people-planning assessments.

▲ *How are selections made?* Every leadership job is filled from a list of well-qualified applicants. The majority of leadership jobs are filled by promotion from within the organization (this holds true for the CEO position as well). To be selected, an individual must be the most qualified person on the slate.

▲ *What happens at People Planning meetings?* A typical agenda includes discussion on organization development, individual development, and bench development. Organization development discussions focus on progress against PepsiCo's key organizational development and change-related initiatives such as inclusion goals. Organizational-health survey results provide important input into this review process. Individual development discussions focus on the progress and development plans of individual executives. These discussions may include data from performance appraisals, 360-degree feedback, and other sources to support discussion on how to help individuals grow. Bench-development discussions focus on talent differentiation, the leadership pipeline for key jobs, and review staffing plans in the context of overall organizational plans.

Divisional People Planning meetings usually occur between April and May each year. The results are reviewed with senior executives between June and July each year.

The Leadership-Competency Model

PepsiCo's leaders recognize that, in order to succeed in the marketplace, the organization needs strong leaders who can set the agenda.

To attract and retain the best people, the organization needs leaders who can take others with them. PepsiCo's leadership model outlines the competencies and behaviors needed to be successful. Inputs into the model include the 360-degree feedback process and the organizational health survey. These provide input into the people objectives and results. Capabilities in certain areas influence decisions about taking on larger roles.

The organization's leadership imperatives have remained consistent for the past fifteen years, though the content of the behaviors that measure these do change from time to time. The three major imperatives are setting the agenda, taking others with you, and doing it the right way. These are supported by various success factors and seventeen related competencies. The success factors are planning, execution, courageous leadership, people development, savvy communication, integrity, and operational excellence. The success factors and leadership competencies form the foundation of the organization's 360-degree feedback process. Every two years, approximately 10,000 managers and executives (including all of the division presidents) receive individualized feedback on the model.

PepsiCo periodically reviews its success factors and leadership competencies to ensure alignment with strategic direction and integration with PepsiCo's values. The reviews also serve to reinforce the importance of manager quality for the future of the organization, enhance focus on demonstrating inclusive behaviors, ensure managers are engaging with employees on key cultural areas (e.g., careers, work/life balance, an inclusive work place), and create a tighter linkage to "living the PepsiCo values."

For example, the organization recently launched an effort to enhance its leadership-competency model. The purpose of the enhancement project is to provide greater differentiation regarding what leadership looks like at different levels in the organization and to update the model to reflect current cultural and strategic business priorities. According to Church, every model (particularly if it is a custom-created model) needs to shift with the organization as its priorities change.

Ties to the Business Strategy

According to Russell, leadership development ties strongly to PepsiCo's business strategy. Previous PepsiCo CEO and chairman of the board Steve Reinemund identified several corporate strategic imperatives (e.g., innovation) each year. Virtually every leadership-development program contains a component devoted to those imperatives. Russell worked very closely with the organization's CEO and chairman, the COO/CFO/CIO, and division presidents to ensure these links between development and business strategy.

Ties to Culture and Values

Although each of the companies that currently make up PepsiCo International had simple beginnings, they were all founded on common values and beliefs. It is these common beliefs that hold the overall organization together. They include an entrepreneurial spirit, passion and perseverance, ownership, people making a difference, staying close to the customer, and leaders with a vision for growth with integrity.

Budget for Leadership Development

Currently, PepsiCo's corporately funded budget for its formal leadership-development programs for senior executives is substantial. Leadership development is a line item in the budget at PepsiCo Corporate. Each year, Russell identifies existing programs that will continue and develops new projects for the year. The budget reflects both of these elements. Nothing is billed back to the divisions for general leadership development. However, if a development program is developed specifically for a functional area, that cost will be billed back to that function.

The annual budget to support the 360-degree feedback process and the organizational-health survey (along with any other new development projects) is shared across the divisions and by Church in the corporate organization-and-management-development function. Additional divisional funding for unique capability needs is also available in the division organization-and-management-development teams.

Building an Integrated Leadership Roadmap

PepsiCo's current approach to training has the business divisions owning the overall training for all employees at all levels, while corporate training overlays this at the executive levels. Formal training programs for PepsiCo executives exist in three areas.

1. *Leadership Training.* This development ties to the leadership-competency model and is offered at key career-transition points for general managers and/or function- and audience-specific leaders as needed. Many of these programs are by invitation only. Leadership programs build skills but, even more important, also shape and elevate expectations and mind-sets.

2. *Functional Excellence Training.* This is professional/technical skill development, consistent with the functional-competency models.

3. *Know the Business/Affiliation Training.* This is targeted at understanding and building affiliation with the business.

As mentioned, the "develop readiness" component of PepsiCo's talent-development process focuses primarily on experiences and on-the-job learning. This requires a culture willing to take some risk, and it means that PepsiCo doesn't always promote the most obvious person.

Other important aspects of developing readiness are coaching, feedback, and mentoring. Research shows that manager quality is very important for developing someone and even more so for retention (people leave managers, not jobs). PepsiCo wants to instill a mind-set in its executives that a big part of their job is developing their people.

The final component is formal education. In today's pressured work environment, learning and development organizations usually don't have time to do something in a formal program sense, so whatever is delivered needs to have a strong impact during the short time people do have to give to training. PepsiCo's people processes not only serve as the foundation and reference point for training but act as an integration tool for employees and managers. It is through the performance-management process that executives, managers, and HR understand where an employee stands on his or her career path and what actions need to be taken (if any) to support future growth, and this can help them build an effective action plan for the employee.

Designing Leadership-Development Programs

PepsiCo's executive leadership programs are almost always developed internally with support from cross-divisional resources as needed. PepsiCo's CEO and chairman, her direct reports, and divisional executives provide insights into the direction of the programs (e.g., links to strategic imperatives). Occasionally, the divisions may call on external vendors to help with the development of division-specific leadership-development programs.

Alignment Across Leadership Programs and Business Strategy

In order to ensure alignment with business strategy, key strategic imperatives are built into the programs at senior levels. Key functional imperatives are built into the functional-leadership programs. PepsiCo's corporate values, however, are built into every program.

Alignment with Talent-Management Systems

According to Church, leader development is strongly integrated with the organization's talent-management (People Planning) process. In fact, Church and Russell both report to the senior vice president of HR.

Leadership-Development Approaches and Tools

PepsiCo leverages a "leaders developing leaders" approach in many of its programs. According to Russell, this is a very powerful approach because PepsiCo's own leaders are best positioned to drive the full benefits of training. According to Paul Russell, vice president of executive learning, "People learn best when they get to learn from someone they really want to learn from." The trick, according to Russell, is to find those people whom others really want to learn from.

At PepsiCo, they are usually the organization's senior leaders. Why? Because these individuals are widely respected, world-class leaders with proven track records at the organization. Russell noted that both former CEOs, Roger Enrico and Steve Reinemund, have stated that the best time they spent was during the week spent developing other leaders. PepsiCo fortunately has a strong legacy of engaging its (senior) leaders to teach other leaders. They do it because it offers them the opportunity to share their personal perspective with the other leaders, allows them to continue to build the skills of those leaders, builds their confidence, and demonstrates support for their growth. In return, they receive greater teamwork and productivity, know the players better (and the participants get to know the leaders better), form a more loyal and motivated team, and encourage closer alignment around vision and key strategic initiatives.

Not only does the leader-developing-leaders approach more fully engage those participating in the programs, but it also helps ensure the transfer of knowledge and skills across generations. Other approaches that address this issue of knowledge transfer and retention include customizing the approaches for every program and consistently using whatever learning strategies will work best for the organization.

All of the above results in training becoming a powerful organization development-and-change leadership tool for PepsiCo to establish the right mind-sets (frame-breaking moments), elevate expectations, gain alignment around a vision, build confidence and express support, and build a team/community of leaders and learners. Examples of some of PepsiCo's leader-led programs include:

▲ The general leadership programs (e.g., Enrico's Executive Leadership: Building the Business and Reinemund's Executive Leadership Program)

▲ Identity-specific programs (e.g., the African American Leadership Forum and the Latino Leadership Forum)

▲ Functional leadership forums for the sales, marketing, R&D, finance, and HR functions

▲ Experiencing PepsiCo (participants in this program hear from heads of most functions, and there's a deep drive from the chairman of PepsiCo International)

▲ Divisional leadership programs across PepsiCo

PepsiCo also uses action learning on business issues in much of its leadership training. For example, in one program, participants had to bring with them an idea to build the business. Not unexpectedly, most people would come with a project they knew they could accomplish. Over the course of the week-long program, however, they would stretch their expectations of themselves and the project and what they could do to accomplish it.

Other approaches used in development programs include action learning on business issues, instructor-led lectures, case-based discussions, experiential learning, job assignment/rotations, mentoring/coaching, special assignments, 360-degree evaluations, performance appraisals, peer feedback, and personal-development workshops.

Key Issues

Key topics or issues emphasized in PepsiCo's development programs include the leadership-competency model, mind-set, change leadership, knowing the business, and personal leadership (via the Corporate Athlete concept). Developed by Jim Loehr and Tony Schwartz, the Corporate Athlete concept posits that the key to sustained performance is to consider the person as a whole. Executives, therefore, are corporate athletes, and if they are to perform at high levels over long periods of time, they must train in the same systematic way that conventional athletes do. This concept addresses integration of the body, emotions, mind, and spirit through a performance pyramid. Each level of the pyramid influences others, and all must be considered in order to achieve optimal performance.

Other topics include building self-awareness (how can I impact the organization and my people?), diversity and inclusion, ethics, specific business issues (strategic imperatives), globalization, strategic planning, innovation, integrity, talent management, visioning, motivation/ empowerment, and values.

Executive Support for Leadership Development

PepsiCo's senior management places a high priority on leader development, which is increasing in terms of importance owing to the aging demographics of the organization's current leadership pool. The CEO and chairman and his or her direct reports, as well as divisional executives, are all involved to some degree in the direction and delivery of various leadership-development programs. In fact, the former CEO devoted up to 25 percent of his time to leadership-development issues.

High Potentials

In order to deliver on its model for sustainable advantage (Figure C.1), PepsiCo needs a talent-management process that supports its two-pronged approach to building leadership capability: (1) broad-based tools that empower people to drive individual development in an inclusive and flexible work environment; and (2) aggressively build bench strength through experience planning for its future leaders.

Over the next five years, a significant number of PepsiCo's current executives across several different levels will be eligible for retirement. According to Church, the organization has a long and strong history of developing and promoting talent from within, but its bench strength is never as deep as it would like. It has a goal of having a two-deep bench for all critical roles, which is sufficient to consistently fill the majority of senior positions from within despite aggressive "poaching" from other organizations. However, PepsiCo's senior leaders and HR organization realize they must build bench now to sustain their growth. They want to develop flexible talent that is "learning agile" and can deal with the unexpected. This means maintaining high standards for both business results and people leadership. The People Planning and Game Planning processes are the primary means for building bench strength.

The HR organization established some core principles around the talent-management model. One of the first is that it wants to integrate the talent-management focus into existing core people processes. Another principle is the need to build capability in the system around experience planning and having a "future back" perspective. Other principles include linking bench-building efforts to the development action plans needed, driving follow-through on experience plans and actions, and involving cross-divisional talent owners for each function before making moves at leadership positions.

Using those principles, PepsiCo recently clarified its talent-development process by updating its talent-development model to focus on three key components: identify, develop, and move. Each of the three elements of talent management focuses on certain tools and approaches. To identify talent, PepsiCo uses assisted assessments and the People Planning process. To develop readiness, the organization uses experiences, on-the-job training, coaching/feedback/mentoring, and formal training. The third component, movement, is based on developmental needs that will allow individuals to accumulate experience and provide a talent pool for the organization's senior-most roles.

Formal training is an important and powerful element of PepsiCo's overall development process. Of course, given the relatively small amount of time any executive can spend in training during the year, the greatest opportunities for affecting his or her development can be achieved by ensuring that he or she receives the right career experiences and assignments, as well as establishing a culture where managers accept coaching and mentoring as critical parts of their roles.

In fact, a primary focus of PepsiCo's talent-management model at the executive level is on cross-divisional talent movement. To create a compelling vision for the future and give leadership capability at PepsiCo teeth, the HR organization realized that it needed to shift perceptions on the part of some senior leaders in the way they were filling jobs (Figure C.2).

Although well known historically for building bench, this emphasis on moving talent sooner and emphasizing a cross-divisional mindset to build experiences represents a desired culture change at PepsiCo.

Figure C.2. Before and after.

From:	To:
Filling open jobs as needed	Creating thoughtful developmental opportunities to build bench
Promoting people to avoid turnover	Stretching the very best talent by giving people the experiences they need
Working with fair and predictable timelines	Talent differentiation and accelerated development where it makes sense
Keeping the best in your own backyard	Facilitating cross-divisional and cross-functional moves to ensure well-rounded future leaders
Stretching the best talent via piling on more work and fewer resources	Ensuring appropriate support and strong teams to ensure success for the business and the individual

Implementing the Successful Leadership-Development Strategy

As part of the annual planning process for the organization and man-agement-development function, each year PepsiCo brings together the corporate and divisional organization-development and training-and-development teams for a two-day alignment meeting. The meeting is led by Church, and the agenda covers such topics as best prac-tices, core process alignment, enhancement or introduction of new conceptual models, research plans, data-based insights, process im-provements, and new strategies. Through recommendations from this meeting, tight links with the broader HR annual planning process with all of the chief personnel officers, and the annual objective-setting process, programs, processes, and systems shift to reflect changing needs.

Implementation of Leadership-Development Programs

Delivery of corporate core programs is consistent and under the con-trol of the vice president of executive learning. Delivery of the divi-sional programs is left to the divisions, and there is inevitably some variation, depending on the business needs of the respective divisions. PepsiCo rarely, if ever, out-sources the delivery of its core programs, although it does sometimes involve external speakers.

PepsiCo's leadership-training programs focus on building strengths, changing mind-sets, and developing capabilities, not remediating weaknesses. Most of the programs are standardized, but there is room for customization through coaching and mentoring.

There are only two full-time employees dedicated to leader-development programs at the corporate level. Several additional full-time employees also exist at the corporate level to support the cross-divisional HR-process agenda (e.g., 360-degree feedback, leadership competencies, and talent-management process).

Evaluating Success

PepsiCo does not use a formal measurement system to evaluate the success of its leader programs. It does not perform many program evaluations outside of an on-site reaction sheet. One major exception, however, is for the CEO's Executive Leadership Program, where participants are required to send an e-mail to the CEO one month following the program outlining what they intend to do differently on their jobs and in their personal lives as a result of having attended the program. Then, at the six-month point, they must write a second e-mail describing what they have actually done differently. The CEO personally reads all of these follow-up e-mails and hosts a conference call to discuss themes with the group and address any common barriers that the participants report having faced in achieving the changes and results they had planned. These personal reports of the impact the program has had on the participants' jobs, careers, and even on their personal lives carry far more weight with the CEO than any participant-reaction forms collected at the end of the program could ever have.

Executive learning is not required to quantify any type of ROI for the leadership-development programs; however, it can point to several changes or improvements in the organization that can be tied to leader-development programs and strategy. These include:

▲ A consistently strong and deep bench of future leaders

▲ Adding to the reputation of the organization

▲ Increased innovation

▲ Changes in behaviors and performance of program participants

▲ The evolution to a culture where "leaders develop leaders" is
increasingly embraced

Other tools used to collect feedback and monitor leadership programs include the organizational-health survey, 360-degree feedback,
and individual development plans.

Communicating Success

Past program participants and the leaders doing the actual teaching
of sessions serve as enthusiastic advocates of the programs and their
impact. The programs are widely known internally to be very engaging, and there is a significant level of pull from clients in the divisions.

Assessing for the Future

Data and insights gleaned from the 360-degree feedback process,
leadership-competency discussions, functional assessments, various
employee profiling efforts, organizational-health surveys, and annual
People Planning discussions and reviews with the CEO and other senior leaders are used to assess current and future needs.

Innovative Aspects

According to Russell, one of the more innovative practices that PepsiCo
has implemented is the corporate athlete concept. Another innovative
practice is the Music Paradigm. Due to PepsiCo's global nature, it has
to be careful not to bring in anything that is uniquely American in
nature.

Lessons Learned

Russell and Church shared the following lessons learned regarding leadership development:

▲ Senior leadership ownership is imperative.

▲ Build a strategy that is linked to other processes, efforts, and cultural initiatives.

▲ Provide the right level of tools and content for the target population.

▲ Customization for the culture is critical.

▲ Leaders-develop-leaders is a powerful training methodology.

PricewaterhouseCoopers

Site Visit Hosts:

▲ Jim Klee, Chief Operating Officer, Learning & Education

▲ Kathryn Kavanagh, Managing Director, Partner Leadership Development, Learning & Education

▲ Dan Goepp, Managing Director, Assurance Practice, Learning & Education

Organization Overview

PricewaterhouseCoopers (PwC) is a professional services firm that provides industry-focused assurance, tax, and advisory services to 85 percent of the *Financial Times* Global 500 organizations. PwC employs more than 130,000 people and operates in 771 cities in 148 countries around the world. In fiscal year 2006, it reported revenue of more than $22 billion.

Unlike a corporation, in which a CEO and leadership team manage the company, PwC is a partnership comprising a global network of firms, each composed of partners. The U.S. firm, on which this case study is based, has over 2,000 partners who act as owners and CEOs. The senior partner is elected by the partners and sets out a strategic direction for the firm. The U.S.-based firm employs approximately 29,000 people and operates in five regions (Northeast, New York Metro, Southeast, Central, and West). In fiscal year 2006, U.S. revenues were almost $7 billion.

PwC was one of *Fortune* magazine's "100 Best Companies to Work For" in 2005, and it was ranked number thirteen in the "Training 100" in 2005. Jim Klee, chief operating officer (COO), Learning & Education, says that although external recognition is good, the firm has not made its improvements for the sake of public accolades but rather to serve the organization. Now that PwC is on the lists, it is driven to continue its efforts to "move to the next level."

> "We take people on tours of our offices, and they look the same—like everyone else's offices. What you can't see on a tour is that it is what is going on in the heads and hearts of our people that matters."
>
> —JIM KLEE, COO, LEARNING & EDUCATION GROUP

PwC operates as a matrix organization. Each partner in the organization is connected to a variety of reporting structures. The U.S. firm has a leadership team that consists of a group of senior partners who are responsible for the lines of service (assurance, taxes, advisory, etc.) and critical functional areas (chief financial officer, etc.). Business units and industry groups reside within each line of service. PwC professionals need both technical expertise related to assurance or tax and industry expertise in order to serve their clients. PwC serves four groups of industries: financial services (FS); consumer and industrial products and services (CIPS); private company services (PCS); and technology, infocomm, and entertainment (TICE).

Each PwC client is owned by one or more partners, and the partners create a hierarchy of project teams that are assigned to serve the client. According to Klee, client time is king at the firm: "When prioritizing their work, people always put the client first. This mind-set is the correct one, but it affects the Learning & Education group's ability to deliver training—anything that takes the PwC professional away from client work must be world-class, worth the investment, and worthy of taking people away from the client focus." Training must directly result in a person's ability to serve the client better. Klee adds, "Basically we produce ideas, and it is the relationship with other people internally and externally that really matters to us."

PwC's employees must be client-focused problem solvers who are innovators, continuous learners, team players, initiative takers, and knowledgeable and skilled advisers. According to Kathryn Kavanagh, managing director, Learning & Education, the accounting world is becoming increasingly regulated, and finding the right balance between innovation and risk taking is increasingly important. PwC is training its leaders to take calculated risks that will not be the wrong kinds of risks but will keep them a creative and evolving organization.

In 1998, PwC was created by the merger of two professional services firms (Coopers & Lybrand and Price Waterhouse). In order to bring the two cultures together, leaders brought employees from both entities together to create a set of values that represented both legacy firms. The values have become embedded in the PwC culture, and employees use them in decision making. The values are shared and promoted with new hires (numbering 8,000 annually), many of whom are recent college graduates. They help these individuals understand the culture of the firm, which is fast-paced; competitive; deadline-driven; professional; team-oriented; increasingly diverse; and local, national, and global.

PwC has an incredible need for knowledge. Clients expect that the firm's employees know more about the business and profession than they do. Legislative and technical changes happen rapidly, and firm leaders, partners, and staff need to sift through information, select what is important, and understand the changes and their implications to ensure they are always current. The firm's client-service philosophy is clearly articulated in its values, which are built on trust, quality, and pride. They include:

▲ Excellence (in innovation, learning, and agility)

▲ Teamwork (involving relationships, respect, and sharing)

▲ Leadership (involving courage, vision, and integrity)

The strength of PwC's culture and the connected thinking of its people help differentiate it from competitors.

Leadership-Development Philosophy

The strength of PwC's partnership culture and the firm values are the central drivers of the firm's leadership-development strategy. PwC views all of its partners as leaders, even those who are not in leadership roles. Leadership-development investments have been strategically focused in two areas: (1) at the partner level, and (2) at key milestones (for example, a program for new managers). The long-term vision is that every key milestone will include a significant leadership experience.

Coaching is fundamentally embedded into all of PwC's leadership-development opportunities. Effective coaching is a broad initiative across the firm at all levels and is part of the culture that is integrated into every process and activity point across the organization. Anyone in the firm is encouraged to give anyone else feedback through the feedback program. At the partner level, it is the responsibility of the primary reporting partner (PRP) to synthesize all of the feedback and performance accomplishments and to balance that with personal knowledge of the partner for whom he or she is a coach to ensure it is meaningful and constructive. Each partner has a primary reporting partner who is responsible for helping develop, support, evaluate, and coach the partner. Each partner receives direction and priorities from his or her line of service leadership and office leadership through what is referred to as an office managing partner (OMP), who resides in the local office and manages office and local market activities. Partners receive feedback from a secondary reporting partner and other commenting partners. The partner also is responsible for serving the needs of a connectivity group (a group of staff members who are assigned to the partner), regulators, and clients. All of these people have an impact on what it means for a partner to be a leader.

The philosophy of leadership development has been to align leaders around the strategic direction of PwC in the United States and enable them to be agile learners who can effectively operate in a constantly changing environment. The firm wants to be known as distinctive, a quality that it believes will lead to profitable growth. So that people will be able to distinguish the firm from its competition, PwC must provide high-quality services and what it terms a "unique people experience" and a "unique client experience." All of the work in the leadership area is connected to becoming distinctive.

Developing Leadership Strategy

PwC has a simple organizational structure. Employees enter the workforce as associates and work their way up to senior associate, manager, and senior manager (or director). The next rung in the ladder is either managing director or partner. Primarily, the managing director position is for individuals with management or deep technical skills who will not become partners, although there are some circumstances where a managing director may be admitted to the partnership. Generally, all partners are client-service partners in some form, and they are responsible for generating revenue. A typical twenty-two-year-old new hire can aspire to achieve partnership by the time he or she is in his or her midthirties.

Historically, when an employee achieved partnership, formal classroom development became less important. According to Klee, partners were often expected to pick up new learnings on their own. Over the last several years, that has changed. Much of the work that the Learning & Education group has done since 2001 has been in nurturing and growing the partners. Klee says, "Partners are hard-working and achievement-oriented. The individuals who make partner are a special breed. They are capable of a lot if left on their own, but they are capable of much more if we can work together with them and if they can help each other." Cooperation and collaboration occurs successfully in pockets of PwC, and one of the goals of the Learning & Education group is to expand those practices throughout the firm.

A partner can gravitate toward one or more of these leadership roles within PwC:

▲ *Client Leaders.* Eighty percent or more of the partners will be in client-facing roles, owning a customer relationship, and indirectly or directly managing teams. The highest level of client leader is the global engagement partner, who leads a global engagement team or serves an international client.

▲ *Business Development Leaders.* This includes approximately 5 percent of the partner population and is growing.

▲ *Organization Leaders.* Five to 10 percent of the partners could assume organization-level leadership roles. For example, there are approximately seventy offices that have an office managing partner or site leader.

▲ *Thought Leaders.* Approximately 5 percent develop their technical expertise and serve as reference for others.

▲ *Functional Leaders.* Less than 1 percent will fall into this category. Such leaders run a service operation such as human capital, marketing, or finance. Everyone in these roles continues to have client responsibilities, so all partners are serving clients.

PwC's leadership-development strategy is driven by the firm's senior partner, who is passionate about developing leaders. He attends all major leadership events. Although ultimately driven by this individual, PwC's leadership-development strategy is inclusive. No one group is responsible for the leadership strategy—it is collaborative and iterative. The strategy was developed and continues to evolve through an inclusive representation of firm leaders from PwC's line-of-service, tax and advisory, leadership-development, human resources (HR), and partner-affairs organizations as well as the U.S. leadership team. (Partner Affairs is a group responsible for managing all matters related to partners including their compensation and partnership agreements.)

Ties to the Business Strategy

PwC's leadership-development strategy is aligned with the firm's "distinctive firm" strategy. Below the strategy, there are business goals in the areas of people, clients, and quality. The leadership strategy grows out of both of these frameworks. All of PwC's key leadership-development programs incorporate a focus on different aspects of people, clients, and quality. Each aspect of the business strategy has a framework that was developed and rolled out firm-wide, and the leadership-development programs are designed to reinforce these frameworks. Through a comprehensive leadership strategy and a related broad human-capital strategy aimed at the "unique people experience" (part of the business goals), the U.S. firm attained its ranking on *Fortune* magazine's "100 Best Places to Work in 2005." Since 2001, the leadership-development strategy has evolved annually as part of the strategic planning and budgeting process.

Ties to Culture and Values

PwC's values serve as a cornerstone for the firm's leadership-development programs, its human-capital initiatives, and its performance measures for all of its employees and partners. There are formal leadership-development programs that focus on alignment with firm strategy and culture, an employee and partner opinion survey conducted twice a year, and a firm-wide coaching model designed to cultivate and reinforce a coaching culture. The firm has documented and published the firm values, which are frequently referred to and embedded in learning programs and work processes for the entry-level associates on up through the partner level. The firm's values of leadership, teamwork, and excellence are also embedded in the recruitment and selection process.

Much of this emphasis has been driven by PwC's senior partner, who, along with his predecessor, had a vision for a distinctive organization and the process of developing partners who are leaders in business, leaders with their people, and leaders with their clients.

The Leadership-Competency Model

The firm's values are the fundamental underpinning of the universal, core competencies by which all staff are measured. PwC has five leadership competencies: (1) developing self and others (coaching), (2) contributing to team success, (3) communicating with impact, (4) having change agility, and (5) demonstrating courage and integrity. Before this list of competencies was implemented, an individual could be extremely successful in the firm without a strong focus on taking care of his or her people. The competencies have been a critical contributor to changing that mind-set.

The universal list of competencies was deployed in 2005 and has had a strong impact in its short life. According to Kavanagh, deploying the competency model was a critical milestone for PwC because the competencies apply across the organization and are directly tied to the values and strategic objective of the firm. Before the competencies were in place, the firm resembled a siloed law firm, with people developing various competencies, some of which originated from the two legacy firms that formed PwC. Staff members today who move around the organization can be evaluated across a consistent set of criteria.

The partner level requires a subset of leadership competencies that align with the universal competencies:

▲ *Partners/Team Leadership.* Effectively directs and influences the collaborative output of others to achieve firm and client goals.

▲ *Coaching and Development.* Focuses on developing and enhancing the skills of others, helps others become more effective, and serves as a resource for others' development efforts.

▲ *Social Respect.* Demonstrates sufficient self-comfort/awareness and awareness of others in business/social situations to gauge impact on others and adapt respectful, effective behaviors in real time.

▲ *Professional and Personal Courage.* Recognizes when a personal stand is professionally necessary and, with seasoned judgment, will address the issue; when necessary, will involve self and others to resolve conflict effectively.

▲ *Learning Agility.* Draws meaning from experiences and, unshackled with pride, modifies approach, based on learned meaning.

PwC developed the competencies with help from both internal and external consultants.

Budget for Leadership Development

Leadership development is highly supported by the firm. The development team submits a strategic plan that outlines the outcomes of the programs, and the budgeting decision is based on the outcomes. According to Kavanagh, if something is believed to be important, PwC typically finds the money to do it. However, this strategy has been a double-edged sword for the Learning & Education team because it means that its work is forever expanding. Ultimately, the lines of service pay for the training, but the expenditures are managed centrally. The Learning & Education budget has stayed flat since 2004, but areas of focus have shifted. Approximately 60 percent of all PwC training is technical.

Building an Integrated Leadership Roadmap

The PwC leadership roadmap is evolving and becoming more robust each year. The roadmap begins with the firm's values and strategy, leadership competencies, and strategic linkages. PwC invests in making the firm a great place to work and an organization in which everyone receives comprehensive coaching and mentoring. One of the strategic links is the firm's Pulse Survey, an employee opinion survey conducted semiannually. The scores on the survey are trending up, and PwC uses the input from the partners and staff to focus its initiatives and activities, which include the following:

▲ *PwC University*. Every two to three years, all partners participate in a significant leadership-development activity that aligns the
partnership with strategic messages and values.

▲ *Quality Lens and Preferred Provider*. These two programs that
focus on partners and managers are affected by the changes brought
on post-Enron and by Sarbanes-Oxley.

▲ *Primary Reporting Partners*. The focus of PwC's Primary Reporting Partner role has shifted to emphasize the developmental portion of the role rather than just the evaluative aspects. Thus, this
program was put together to help the partners navigate these new
responsibilities and gain skills and tools to use in coaching their colleagues.

▲ *Starting Out Able and Ready (SOAR)*. This is a three-year program for newly admitted partners.

In addition, there is a coaching curriculum that spans all levels
of the organization. Leadership-development programs are designed
with career progression in mind. Each program concentrates on a
specific area of an employee's career ladder. Most of these initiatives
concentrate on the partner level, and although they do not represent
all of the firm's efforts, they are representative of leadership development and the ways it is helping to evolve PwC culture. Let's look at
each of these programs.

PwC University

In 2001, partner development was top-of-mind for PwC's management committee. The firm had undergone tremendous change due to
the merger, and a specific PwC culture had not been developed. To
address this, the U.S. Management Committee and the Learning &
Education group developed the concept of PwC University.

After reviewing several options, the team commissioned Duke
Corporate Education (Duke CE), rated highly for worldwide customized learning, to help in program development. PwC's leadership
training had to be customized and had to address the issues in the

organization. It could not be "off the shelf." Together, the two organizations developed key themes that would drive content and design. Their challenge was to create a partner-development environment that is:

▲ A continuous learning environment (not just an event)

▲ State-of-the-art, distinctive, and "at the edge"

▲ Firmly grounded in the business and the strategy

▲ Designed to focus on partner behaviors and values

▲ Intended to build culture and to energize the partnership

▲ Centered on a residential experience

The development team included accountants and technical professionals, typically not the type of individuals who would design a distinctive, at-the-edge program. However, the team was willing to take risks to develop a program that made a difference in the culture. At the time, the partners were feeling neglected because they were often not involved in making the decisions that affected them. Therefore, a vital part of the training had to involve giving partners an understanding of their role and a voice to express their problems and concerns.

The sessions involved "experiences" (i.e., metaphorical, experiential learning situations) in the mornings and related teachings in the afternoons. It removed the partners from their daily business lives in which they are "the experts" into "learning experiences" in which all partners are equally inexpert and outside their comfort zones. The training centered on the values of the firm (leadership, excellence, and teamwork) and critical attributes of client service (trust and quality). The goals of the training were to:

▲ Bring additional quality into the business

▲ Take responsibility for managing the day-to-day people experience and creating a productive work environment

▲ Act as one firm

▲ Build great relationships

▲ Create a sales and business-development mind-set

▲ Be a successful partnership

▲ Drive the client-service attributes, relationship-development attributes, and core values throughout the organization

However, the Learning & Education team realized that the goals could not be met through lectures; they had to be inculcated through experiences. Having partners experience how it feels to meet the goals became part of the delivery strategy.

The "experience" brought partners from both merged firms together to work through their "legacy baggage." One way they accomplished this was through an experience of changing tires on a race car where the partners acted as part of a NASCAR team and learned to work the way teams do in a racing-pit crew. The debriefing that followed allowed partners to relate the experience back to the consulting world. The partners were fully engaged because it was fun and out of the ordinary, and the experience was easily related to their work experience

Another "experience" used judo to help the partners experience professionalism, focusing on the moment, and working through issues strategically and tactically. The pilot program was held at a central site. It was successful, not because it was perfectly integrated but because the 120 partners from across the country with different backgrounds realized they were in business together. They ended the pilot program with a debriefing in which they verbalized how the program had changed their outlook. After the team had completed a few of these PwC University programs, leadership development reached a tipping point, and partners began to seek out places in the sessions. The program was delivered seventeen times, each session composed of approximately 150 partners each. Approximately 95 percent of the partners attended this "experience."

Since the inception of the PwC University experiences, the learning team has since delivered PwC University 2, another experience for all U.S. partners that is described further in this case. The Learning & Education group designed the sessions in partnership with Duke CE. Approximately fifteen PwC staff were required to run a PwC University 1 session, and it required thirty additional external part-time faculty.

The development team knew that the sessions would be more successful if senior management was deeply involved, and so the decision was made that the firm's senior partner and two other U.S. Management Committee members would attend each session. On day one, the session began with a welcome and introductions, a discussion on firm strategy, Socratic dialogue, and "Making It Happen." On days two and three, the participants engaged in activities surrounding either "Becoming a Great Place to Work" or "World-Class Client Relationships." On day four, the session concluded with a Habitat for Humanity experience and sessions called "Teaming to Win" and "Power of Story," as well as a closing dinner.

One offshoot of the PwC University program is the Extended Leadership Team Experiences program. The program began in 2002 and continues through today. The program consists of quarterly two-day sessions that bring the top 100 leaders together. The program is based on a specific leadership topic, and sessions have covered coaching, diversity, aligning the partnership around strategic messages, and involving others beyond the extended leadership team in the firm. These topics are determined through a series of visioning sessions conducted periodically with the firm's top leadership.

In 2005 and 2006, a PwC University 2 experience was delivered. Unlike University 1, which was conducted at a national level, PwC University 2 is delivered in seventeen local markets (localities where work is done). Each of the office managing partners plays a significant leadership role in the University 2 experience. This allows the program to target specific market needs while maintaining an overall consistent framework. Prior to the session, work is done with each office/market managing partner and a consultant to identify the key challenges that are keeping the market from becoming distinctive. Each session has had a different tone, as dependent on the skill level of the office managing partner, and helps participants determine the action plans and accountability that will increase PwC's distinction in their market. The result of each session is a set of commitments they make to each other concerning their market.

The advantages of the University 2 program are that it allows the local offices to discover areas where they are distinct and employ those attributes more consistently across all areas. It also encourages change to be embedded in daily work, making "things that matter," such as coaching, a higher priority and therefore more part of the culture.

Because the participants in University 2 work harder and do not have as many fun activities, Learning & Education has more difficulty attracting participation for the three days. However, because leadership commitment is as deep for University 2 as it was for University 1, a total of 90 percent of the partners have also attended University 2 at the time of our site visit (mid-2006).

Quality Lens

The highly publicized corporate scandals that have occurred over the past few years challenged many of the partners in PwC to question whether they were still able to bring quality and trust to their client relationships. For example, before the collapse of Enron, the industry had become commoditized. Professionals were simply checking boxes after they had completed auditing tasks, and jobs were given to the low-cost provider. Enron taught clients that they needed to ask the auditors not only whether they had the right numbers but also how they knew they had the right numbers.

After Enron, PwC's leadership had to return to a focus on the quality of both the audit and the conversations with the clients. Quality Lens 1 was created in 2002 by designers who understood that the industry had six to nine months to prove it could still be noble and clients could trust the audit and the auditor. Its purpose was to teach participants to form a point of view, communicate difficult messages, and increase trust in relationships.

Quality Lens focuses on assurance and quality practices. It was created to help partners work together so that the company and individuals will not be faced with the corruption that can occur when individuals act on their own. PwC's message is "consult, consult, consult." No matter how much pressure partners are under, they are required as owners of the company to consult with one another directly.

Quality Lens is built on the PwC University 1 model. Its objective is to develop technical expertise through metaphorical experiences. For example, participants accompanied doctors on medical rounds. They learned from doctors how to diagnose a patient and how to deliver a difficult message to a person. The program included improvisation with professional actors and other metaphorical experiences.

During the first year of Quality Lens, it was paralleled by a program called the New Manager Experience that helped managers address the challenge of quality. Owing to the program's success, the firm decided to bring partners and managers together for the second version of Quality Lens (Quality Lens 2), which involved learning by doing. Its purpose was to help participants learn how to conduct process auditing and recognize fraud. The delivery team gave the participants sample work papers and had them listen to interviews conducted with CEOs (played by actors). By observing these simulations, the participants determined what type of conversations they would have to have with the clients to ensure that fraud was not occurring.

The Learning & Education team also developed innovative activities about detection and deception. In one exercise, one member of a three-person team steals a $100 bill. The team is allowed to keep the money if its members can survive an interview conducted by the participants who try to detect who took the money. Participants learn to focus not only on what is said, but also on how it is said.

Quality Lens 3, designed in 2004, was tactical; it focused on the specifics of the audit methodology. The newer partners accepted the training well, as did the veteran partners who were performing audits in the 1970s. They were pleased that auditing was reverting to a holistic approach. However, the Learning & Education team did discover that partners in the middle bracket had a difficult time with the process approach.

Over recent years, Quality Lens has grown more technical, and the

Learning & Education group has been asked to bring back some of the nontechnical core behaviors such as diversity training, coaching skills, and reinforcing culture.

Quality Lens works in conjunction with PwC University, reinforcing its messages.

Preferred-Provider Program

Leadership training helps partners realize that, throughout their careers, they must learn and grow to meet the changing needs of the environment. The fallout from Enron and the implementation of Sarbanes-Oxley regulations required PwC and all accounting firms to change their business models to a great degree. This affected many of their partners, who found themselves having to learn how to work differently. To help them in this transition and the redeployment of its partners, PwC's Learning & Education group developed the Preferred Provider Program.

PwC sees itself as having two channels of business now. Channel one is defined as its traditional audit business. It is trying to grow channel two, which involves a consulting relationship with a company that does not use PwC for audits. Under the Preferred Provider Program, some partners are now developing expertise in selling to and serving channel two clients. The partners who remain in channel one can focus extensively on the quality of the audit.

Coaching Skills for Primary Reporting Partners

As previously stated, the primary reporting partner (PRP) is the person to whom partners in a specific industry or geographical area report for evaluative and developmental purposes. The PRP is both an evaluator and a coach. In recent years, the firm has found itself facing leadership challenges in handling the dynamic of young partners with only five years of experience moving into the role of primary reporting partner and trying to coach and mentor people with fifteen to twenty years of partner experience. PwC has approximately 350 reporting partners. During the past three years, the firm has worked to find the correct number of people who can play this role effectively.

Ideally, a PRP will mentor and coach five to seven individuals; however, some primary reporting partners coach only one partner while others serve ten to eleven partners—a larger number that creates challenges for that individual.

Through feedback from the first session of PwC University 1, the firm learned that partners did not feel supported in their growth and development. As a result, firm leaders began three initiatives: (1) a critical review of the income system for the partners, (2) a redefinition of the role of the primary reporting partners, and (3) an investment in increasing the coaching skills of the primary reporting partners. In 2003 the firm offered a program called Coaching Skills for Primary Reporting Partners to every PRP with five or more partners to coach. The two-day program helped the primary reporting partners understand their roles and practice their coaching skills. Each PRP was assigned an external executive coach who worked with him or her during the session and was available for three months following the session. The partners also engaged in role play with professional actors to handle difficult partner-to-partner conversations. Here are two examples:

1. A high-performing partner has an Achilles' heel that will hold her back from long-term success. The primary reporting partner needs to motivate her while simultaneously helping her to recognize the blind spot.
2. A partner has reached a career plateau and will not be moved to a higher responsibility level (higher responsibility levels equate to more partner shares, a higher income, and status as a partner).

The external executive coaches deliver this role-playing fishbowl session to ten or fewer people. The participants are able to start and stop the action, do conversations over, and learn from each other. The development team selected the external coaches carefully. Duke CE helped with the initial screening, and each prospective coach was individually interviewed.

The program has been successful, and partner feedback ranks interaction with the external coaches and the role play higher than any

other part of the program. Firm leaders are strong program support-
ers and allow themselves to participate and "fail" along with everyone
else. The program is required for all new primary reporting partners.
Currently, the firm asks that even PRPs with only a few partners to
coach go through the session. Developers of the program have seen
improvement in the scores that partners give their primary reporting
partners for the skill on which they are evaluated.

As of 2006, the original coaching-skill training for primary reporting partners has an extension, a coaching workshop. One hundred
partners recently participated in a four-hour workshop leading up
to the 2006 evaluation process. The partners presented the personal
challenges that they knew they would be dealing with in real life. They
practice writing and delivering the feedback. During the workshop,
the participants practice with each other, not with professional actors.
However, the team doubts that the participants would be able to role
play as well if they had not worked with the professional actors during
the main course. The proceedings of the workshop are confidential,
which helps the partners maintain trust and encourages experimentation.

The Starting Out Able & Ready Program

A strategic focus on young partners began in 2003, when the demographics of partnership began to shift with 50 percent of partners
having fewer than seven years tenure as partner. The Starting Out
Able & Ready (SOAR) Program is a three-part series designed to accelerate the development of individuals during their first three partnership years. The program addresses the mind-set shift from being an
employee to being an owner of the company, because partners need
to understand that they have the power to determine the success and
culture of the firm.

SOAR is delivered through a combination of external world-class
faculty, high-performing senior partners, and leadership partners (including board members or partners). A maximum of forty-eight participants are in a single SOAR group. SOAR has three phases, each
lasting one year.

Phase 1 begins with the take-off event—an individual assessment session with an executive coach. Then, during a three-day residential meeting, they are observed by faculty as they are engaged in various activities, and they meet one-on-one with an executive coach. The final activity of the three days is the development of a two- to three-year development plan that outlines where they would like to go as partners.

Before this program, executive coaches were not used routinely; they coached individuals only for the purpose of solving problems. Partners are beginning to realize that executive coaches do more than help solve problems—they also help take advantage of major opportunities. The process is increasing the importance of coaching in the firm.

For each partner, the executive coaches synthesize psychometric, client, senior partner, peer/upward feedback, and behavioral data. They identify significant patterns and themes within each partner's data; they assist partners in prioritizing development areas and creating development plans. Primary psychometric data includes: (A) FIRO–B (Fundamental Interpersonal Relationship Orientation–Behavior), which measures how individuals behave toward other people and how they expect others to behave toward them; (B) Learning Agility, which measures the ability to learn from experiences and apply what is learned to new situations; and (C) Ambiguity Architect, which measures the ability to handle uncertainty.

Partners are also measured on observable problem-solving experiences, role-play experiences related to situations requiring professional courage, participation in small-group discussion, participation in one-on-one coaching, and peer coaching/contributions. During a final session following the residential experience, the new partner, the executive coach, and the new partner's primary reporting partner meet, and the executive coach hands off the coaching and mentoring responsibilities to the primary reporting partner. Only a small percentage of partners request additional coaching after the three months that is provided.

Phase 2 focuses on building connections (relationships) with clients, peers, and staff. During a two-day event, the partner receives personalized instruction related to influence through negotiation and conflict management. Skills include conducting difficult conversations and building trust, and there are activities designed to build those skills. Partners are videotaped and critiqued during these activities. Additionally, an FBI hostage negotiator helps them practice demonstrating empathy.

Studies show that the most distinctive attribute of a partner in one of the Big Four consulting firms is his or her ability to build and maintain relationships. Phase 2 results in a plan to build personal networks and long-term relationships.

Phase 3 examines the road ahead. It focuses on examining the types of career paths open to partners who learn about the additional opportunities that they can gravitate toward. Some are interested in organizational leadership, and some in client leadership. Coaching and guidance about their career options are provided. It also explores ways to achieve work/life balance. The firm is currently redesigning this phase and debating whether it would like to identify certain partners as having key talent and high potential.

Alignment Across Leadership Programs and Business Strategy

Before each leadership-development program is rolled out, the design team consults with a committee of designated leader-partners who serve as a strategic sounding board to ensure alignment around the correct messages.

Leadership-Development Approaches and Tools

The firm uses a variety of tools and approaches in its leadership programs, including action learning on business issues; Internet; classroom, instructor-led lectures; intranet; classroom, case-based discussion; job assignments/rotations; leadership and/or facilitation of one or more communities of practice; mentoring/coaching; facilitated small-group discussions; electronic performance-support systems; special assignments; experiential learning; teleconferencing; and access to external executive coaches.

PwC's leadership programs address a variety of topics, including building self-awareness, quality, change management, customer service, specific business issues, diversity, specific strategic initiatives, ethics, strategic planning, innovation, integrity, talent management, interpersonal behavior skills, values, leadership styles, visioning, and motivation/empowerment. An increased focus on coaching is a key issue that brings the entire organization together. The firm is concentrating on developing coaching skills in a wide variety of individuals and is making coaching part of everyday activity. When employees are open and look to one another for help and advice, the firm is safer from fraud and scandal.

Executive Support for Leadership Development

PwC's U.S. Management Committee (the organization's highest-level leadership team) is highly involved in all decisions regarding partner leadership development and involved to an appropriate degree in setting the vision of leadership development at all other levels. All members of this committee demonstrate their support through attending key partner programs where they speak, lead, and are highly involved in the discussions and, in some cases, participate along with other partners and participants. At other levels in PwC, the appropriate leaders attend key leadership-development programs to ensure the right messages are getting across in terms of organization strategy as well as making themselves available to the participants for Q&A around any topic.

Implementing the Successful Leadership-Development Strategy

PwC's business strategy changes as its business needs change, which in turn causes them to periodically reexamine their leadership strategy. The organization constantly reevaluates the leadership skills required to accomplish the business strategy and adjusts the leadership strategy accordingly. This occurs in collaboration with the organization's highest level of leadership and leadership from the learning organization.

Training is redesigned and updated frequently to align with leadership messages and business shifts, and the PwC University Experience is different every three years. Leadership training follows a systemic approach that is built incrementally year to year. Most programs are delivered nationally or regionally without variation because the consistency of message is critical.

Governance

The Learning & Education group is part of PwC's human-capital organization and employs 250 individuals, a small subset of which focuses only on leadership development. Learning & Education is affected by PwC's matrix structure because it has to satisfy a wide range of stakeholders. The complexity of the firm causes interesting organizational dynamics. Employees continually have to weigh and assess priorities. One employee may be asked to devote his time, effort, and energy to a line-of-service leader, an industry leader, and office-level manager simultaneously.

Leadership-development teams include both internal and external resources. The internal group develops the vision for the programs, and external vendors do most of the design and delivery work. The partnership with Duke Corporate Education is strong and has been involved with many leadership projects.

Evaluating Success

Like many organizations, PwC is very measurement-oriented. Kavanagh says, "We are masters of acting on the things that are measured." One measurement tool is the Pulse Survey, a biannual employee opinion survey. The survey measures level of job satisfaction, quality of programs, and behavior change (among other things). The survey questions were developed internally and had not changed substantially until a few new items were added in 2004. PwC tracks the survey results over time. Top leaders focus on the survey results and use them to prioritize improvements.

PwC has seen great progress at all staff levels in a wide range of areas, and the percentage of the employees responding to the survey increases each year. In fact one result of the survey and resulting actions taken by leaders has been a turnaround of negative perceptions (lack of trust) on the part of employees who now see the commitment from leadership to make changes in the firm.

All PwC learning programs are evaluated on the reaction level. Annually, the learning-effectiveness team helps each group create a plan for higher-level evaluations for certain programs. The team also uses a success-case method in which it surveys the entire group and conducts follow-up conversations with the high and low scorers.

A learning-effectiveness team resides in the Learning & Education group. This team is responsible for identifying evaluation tools and helping to create an evaluation or an assessment (a measure of knowledge level) for every program at every level. The team consists of six individuals with backgrounds in assessment, measurement, and statistical analysis. Several have Ph.D.'s in organizational psychology.

Communicating Success

Successes resulting from the leadership-development programs are communicated in a variety of ways. For example, PwC's chairman and senior partner has a weekly conversation with the firm's partners, and values are part of that communication. Additionally, there's a monthly communication to the staff that includes values and actions to take on survey results.

Assessing for the Future

As part of the strategic-planning process, development needs of the future are identified. Typically, these are targeted out on a three- to five-year future horizon. Both Learning & Education and firm leadership work together on this process.

Innovative Aspects

According to members of the Learning & Education team, some of PwC's innovative leadership-development practices include the SOAR program, the primary reporting partner training, the use of metaphorical experiences, role playing with professional actors, and follow-up and integration measures conducted after the SOAR take-off event.

Critical Success Factors and Lessons Learned

Critical success factors for PwC's leadership-development strategy include:

▲ Involving leadership in training

▲ Building on successes (which creates an atmosphere in which employees want to learn rather than being forced to participate in programs)

▲ Making strategic choices that will result in high impact

▲ Integrating training with other processes such as coaching

▲ Realizing the process of building a fully integrated road map is long

Creating an atmosphere of trust in a virtual environment is a key challenge for the firm. Partners must trust one another, even when they cannot meet face-to-face. To achieve trust, the firm has identified what it means to be a partner and the qualities that one partner can expect when interacting with another. The compensation system helps to increase trust because it is based on the profitability of the firm as a whole. Partners become willing to work for another's success.

Trust is also important in an environment where a distinction is made between partners and the staff. Leaders in PwC continue to be uncertain whether a staff member would have the courage to be open and honest if the information were shared with partners. Learning & Education intends to build activities into future leadership training to facilitate the development of trust among levels.

The firm is considering training some HR professionals to help with some coaching tasks and is increasing coach training across the organization.

Two key factors in PwC's current success are (1) replacing change-resistant partners in leadership roles (some through retirement) and (2) changing the reward and recognition system. Partners should be rewarded when their staffs have a manageable level of overtime and are able to take vacations.

Kavanagh notes that leadership development is a journey that never ends. Patience is essential. Teams should select strategic places to make an initial investment and build on the investment in the future.

Washington Group International

Site Visit Hosts:

▲ Jennifer A. Large, Vice President, Integrated Staffing and Talent Management

▲ Stephen P. Muller, Director, Employee Development

▲ Larry L. Myers, Senior Vice President, Human Resources

Organization Overview

Washington Group International (Washington Group) provides engineering, construction, and management solutions to businesses and governments worldwide. Headquartered in Boise, Idaho, with more than $3 billion in annual revenues, the organization employs approximately 24,000 people around the world and holds leading positions in defense, energy and environment, industrial/process, infrastructure, mining, and power markets. The organization engineers, constructs, and manages industrial facilities, power plants, clean-air systems, transmission and distribution systems, oil and gas plants, dams and water-treatment facilities, roads, bridges, rail systems, airports, and other infrastructure. It is making the world a safer place through its environmental management and defense services, including operating national laboratories, managing hazardous waste, destroying chemical and other weapons, and providing security systems for border and port security. The organization helps the world harness natural resources by mining everything from coal and precious metals to zinc, phosphorus, bauxite, and other minerals.

Washington Group's main customers are government agencies (including the U.S. Department of Defense, Department of Energy, and state transportation departments) and businesses ranging from power utilities and oil and gas companies to leading organizations across industries including Caterpillar, Kraft, Monsanto, Amgen, and General Motors. Other organizations in similar markets include Fluor, Bechtel, Jacobs Engineering, Shaw Group, Parsons Corporation, CH2M Hill, Parsons Brinckerhoff, and Granite Construction.

Washington Group was cited in 2005 by Hewitt and Associates as one of the top twenty U.S. companies for developing leaders. Washington Group has two key priorities: safe operations throughout its business and attracting, developing, and retaining top talent. The organization believes that investing in its people will create value for shareholders. Talent planning and development has been a driving element of the Washington Group philosophy for the last several years.

Developing Leadership Strategy

Washington Group's leadership-development strategy is built into its mission statement, values, recognition programs, and internal and external communications. According to organization representatives, it is best articulated in the organization's threefold mission of "developing people, achieving superior performance, and sustained profitability." More specifically, "developing people" refers to promoting professional growth and development opportunities in a fair and stimulating environment. "Performance" refers to developing profitable new businesses and executing with best-in-class performance by aggressively managing quality, cost, schedule, and safety. Finally, "profitability" means producing profits and cash flows that yield 10 percent annual increases in earnings per share and returns on invested capital that exceed cost of capital. The organization's underlying belief is that performance and profitability flow naturally when talented people are challenged and rewarded for their efforts. Because "The Washington Way" encourages the use of similar processes, procedures, and approaches to doing work, people can find challenging assignments throughout the organization.

Washington Group's leadership strategy is twofold. The organization strives to provide the best engineering, construction, and management solutions for its customers. It does this through strong leadership practices that begin at the top of the organization. In turn, the organization encourages employees to be well trained and self-motivated and to accept personal responsibility for their professional development and growth.

Leadership development at Washington Group is a responsibility shared among a number of key internal stakeholders. Although the primary responsibility for strategy development lies at the corporate level, the organization's six business units provide input and, in most cases, dedicated resources that focus on the development of talent. Leadership-development initiatives are derived from business-unit strategic plans as they are rolled into the organization's overall strategic initiatives. The organization's integrated staffing and talent-management function analyzes these initiatives and proposes leadership-development strategies that are reviewed and approved by the office of the chairman (the organization's four-member senior leadership team). This group is not only kept apprised of progress, but it is also directly involved in leadership-development initiatives.

At the working level, employees experience this strategy through their management team, in which individual goals and objectives are set to ensure that employees' work is aligned with business-unit and work-group goals and objectives. This takes place through the development-planning process (known as the Development Planner) during which managers and employees set goals, measure progress against those goals, and set meaningful professional-development objectives. Washington Group refers to this as a "three-way partnership" in which the organization provides development resources, managers provide advice and coaching, and the employee takes personal responsibility for his or her performance and development. Ideally, the at-least-once-a-year development-planning process focuses on using an employee's strengths to develop his or her weaknesses.

When this approach was developed about five years ago, Washington Group recognized that it would be asking many of its managers and employees to take responsibility for professional growth in a way that would be unfamiliar to them. One of the ways it addressed this potential problem was to provide development tools directly to its workers. An example is an electronic publication called YOU.inc ("you-dot-inc") in which the company encouraged employees to think of themselves as individual companies selling their services back to Washington Group. The publication contained upbeat articles on topics such as how to communicate clearly, how to set goals, and how to get feedback from a reluctant manager. It also focused on nontraining-related development ideas—those things employees could do on the job to learn new skills. Directly and indirectly, YOU.inc improved communications and resulted in buy-in for the organization's leadership-development strategy.

In addition to individual development efforts, the organization often looks for business-unit initiatives that can be elevated and turned into corporate-wide initiatives. For example, a college graduate rotation program in one organization was redesigned, refocused on developing new project managers, and implemented organization-wide in 2005. Individuals selected to be in the program were both existing and newly hired employees. The program more than doubled in size during 2006.

Ties to the Business Strategy

As mentioned earlier, business-unit strategies feed corporate strategies (and visa versa) around which leadership-development strategies are formed. These strategies become the basis of the Employee Development Strategic Plan, a document that shapes and articulates specific tactical actions to develop leaders. The plan emphasizes development in three areas:

1. Leadership and management skills (the premier focus in 2006)
2. Technical skills (e.g., project management, business development, and safety)
3. Business skills

The plan contains both near-term actions to be completed in 2006 and longer-term actions covering several years.

Ties to Culture and Values

Because Washington Group believes that a successful approach to professional development is a three-way partnership among the employee, the manager, and the organization, it communicates them in that manner. The organization's threefold mission of "people, performance, and profitability" drives the organizational culture. When these terms are used, "people" is always placed first as a symbol of the importance of developing talent in an organization. Further, Washington Group values (integrity, candor, safety, diversity, accountability and responsibility, cooperation and efficiency, and competence and professional behavior) are clearly articulated and routinely included as topics of discussion during its formal training and development programs. It is the employee's responsibility to take active ownership of his or her development with, as mentioned earlier, the support of the management team and organization.

The Leadership-Competency Model

Washington Group defines success in terms of competencies and results. The organization's twelve competencies (called business skills) establish the basis for hiring, developing, retaining, and promoting employees.

Shortly after emerging from financial restructuring about five years ago, Washington Group faced significant people-related issues, the most striking being the existence of multiple cultures and performance-appraisal systems and the lack of a cohesive way to develop talent. The organization assessed a number of competency models including those from Lominger Limited, British Nuclear Fuels, the Department of Defense, General Electric, The Center for Creative Leadership (CCL), and Motorola, and benchmarked them. The benchmarking process resulted in the organization's selecting twelve business skills that would form the basis of appraising and developing employees. They are as follows: acts with integrity; builds collaborative relationships; communicates clearly; encourages change; fosters diversity of people, ideas, and action; gets results; influences effectively; knows the business; pursues self-development; sets high expectations; shows resilience and flexibility; and thinks ahead.

While the organization acknowledged that the skills list is somewhat brief when compared to other competency models, Washington Group wanted to keep its approach to a single development process streamlined, focusing on simple development tools that could be expanded as needed by individual managers and employees. For example, a 360-degree feedback process used for senior managers includes more than sixty competencies that amplify the twelve business skills above. It should be noted that these twelve business skills are applicable to all employees regardless of job responsibility or position.

The business skills form the basis of the Development Planner (discussed at the beginning of this section) and are described, in detail, in the organization's publication "One Dozen Business Skills for Career Success," published and distributed to employees in both hard and electronic formats. Because the booklet contains references to current books and publications, it is updated yearly to ensure that resources are actually available.

A fully electronic version of the Development Planner and business skills booklet are being created and will enable employees to link development needs to online and classroom courses through an automated enrollment process. For example, if "fostering diversity" is a developmental need, a list of resources, including online and classroom courses, will appear, permitting the planned development activity to be tracked and monitored. Once again, individual efforts are closely tied to corporate goals and objectives and are part of the "people development culture" prevalent at Washington Group.

Budget for Leadership Development

Over the past four years, Washington Group has invested more than $200 million in employee development. This equates to more than 4.2 million hours of training. Approximately 50 to 60 percent of the training is technical and focuses on safety, technical skills, and operational excellence. (Owing to the highly complex, technical nature of some of its contracts, Washington Group often provides training in all aspects of a particular process such as the destruction of chemical weapons. In these cases, costs are reimbursed by customers.) The remaining 40 to 50 percent of training is leadership and professional-development training.

In 2006, $60 million was spent on training, including $2 million on tuition reimbursement. Of the $60 million, the integrated staffing and talent-management budget is about $4.5 million. Washington Group sets it training budgets based on client requirements and by costing the strategic initiatives that are part of the employee-development strategic plan. It should be noted that, although *training* is often used synonymously with *employee development*, the organization actively encourages its employees and managers to think much more broadly than formal classroom training as a means to develop knowledge and skills.

Washington Group is a world leader in developing and certifying safety-trained supervisors, which reflects the organization's commitment to creating a safe work environment. This training initiative resulted, in part, in Washington Group and its largest business unit being named among America's seventeen safest companies by *Occupational Hazards* magazine (in 2004 and 2005).

Training on technical and nontechnical subjects is also available online through two e-learning platforms: KnowledgeWire, provided through EduNeering (a Princeton, New Jersey, organization) and MindLeaders, based in Dublin, Ohio. The total number of courses offered online exceeds 500. These courses are available in up to thirteen languages.

Washington Group has been questioned by analysts about its investment in professional development and how that investment affects earnings per share. The organization strongly believes that developing its intellectual capital—and, thus, a sustainable business—is a critical factor in achieving growth rate targets. This reflects its strong commitment to people development and the belief of the organization's senior leadership that taking "the long view" (looking ten to twenty years into the future) when it comes to developing people will build long-term business success.

Building an Integrated Leadership Roadmap

Washington Group has an integrated organizational structure as shown in Figure E.1. The fourteen members of the executive team are the office of the chairman (the president and heads of business develop-

Figure E.1. Washington Group's integrated organizational structure.

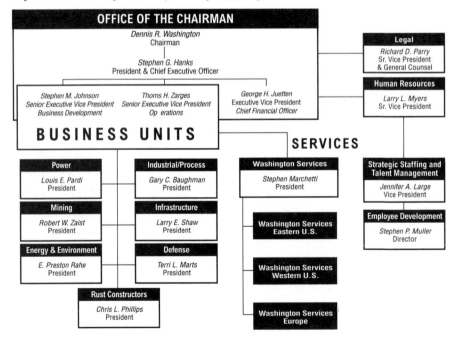

ment, operations, and finance), the heads of the human resources and legal departments, presidents of the six business units, and the heads of Washington Services and Rust Constructors. The office of the chairman, as well as the entire executive team, routinely meets to discuss leadership development during quarterly business reviews. The six business units were intentionally created to serve specific markets but act in a way that shares talent in a flexible manner designed to support the business and employees' professional growth.

Alignment Across Leadership Programs and Business Strategy

The leadership-development strategy emerged in 2001 as key internal stakeholders met with the office of the chairman to discuss the importance of developing leaders and to create an actionable strategy to strengthen the organization's leadership bench strength.

The leadership-development pyramid (Figure E.2) coordinates and aligns with Washington Group's business and is the organization's leadership roadmap. The pyramid has several components. The gray, outer segments of the pyramid represent the foundation of the Washington Group development strategy: experiential learning; stretch assignments; and coach, mentor, and peer learning. Of note is that the outer bands—the foundation—do not focus on training because Washington Group believes that training is only one way to gain additional knowledge—and not necessarily the most effective way. The organization strongly believes that real-world, activity-based learning helps employees gain a clearer, more results-focused way of dealing with actual problems. The central areas in the pyramid LEAP, Leaders Forum, and What's Your Point? represent the sequence of leadership-development events for senior-level high potentials. The other central areas are events for high potentials in less senior positions.

Although the organization has numerous development programs, three are highlighted here.

1. *Leadership Excellence and Performance* (LEAP). This program was began in 2002 as a selective program for high potentials who showed leadership promise and the ability to move into more respon-

Figure E.2. Washington Group's leadership-development pyramid.

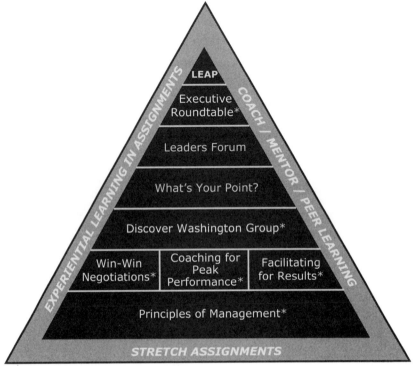

New in 2005 - 2006

sible positions. It has included over sixty participants to date. The focus of the project is on individual feedback and development, 360-degree assessments, personal action plans, and exposure to a variety of business segments. All participants are assigned mentors, who are available throughout the year. Each is also assigned a sponsor from the executive team.

LEAP has been very successful, in part, because the CEO is personally committed to the project and permits participants to shadow him or her throughout the year. Along with support from the CEO, the top six leaders are also modeling the behavior necessary to have a strong leadership-development program.

2. *Leaders Forum.* See Figure E.3. This program is the cornerstone of the leadership-development process. It is a fifty-hour course,

Figure E.3. The Leaders Forum.

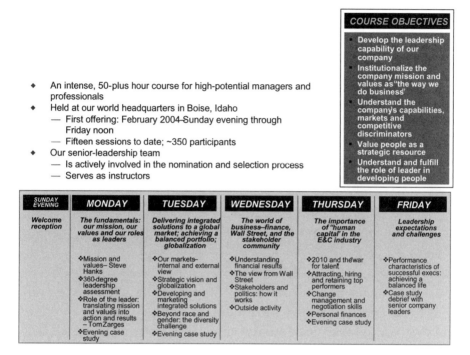

which was first offered in February 2004. More than 400 participants have attended one of the sixteen sessions to date. The course objectives are:

▲ To develop the leadership capability of the organization

▲ To institutionalize the organization's mission and values as "the way we do business"

▲ To understand the organization's capabilities, markets, and competitive discriminators

▲ To value people as a strategic resource

▲ To understand and fulfill the role of leader in developing people

Participants are selected by senior leadership and are exposed to the organization's philosophy, key business issues, and approach to doing business. Senior leaders are also personally involved in the delivery of course content. The chief financial officer, for example, uses a *Jeopardy!*-like electronic board game to help participants understand financial results. Although not intended to be a cultural change intervention at its inception, the Leaders Forum has shifted the way managers and others view the organization and their roles in leading others.

3. *Executive Roundtable.* This program was designed to help high-performing leaders develop "strategic agility," or the ability to think broadly and creatively and to adapt to ever-changing input and environmental factors. The Roundtable uses a theme taken from Lewis and Clark's remarkable journey to find the Northwest Passage from Saint Louis to the Pacific Ocean. During their adventure, the explorers faced daily opportunities to practice strategic agility. In the first two and a half days, participants receive feedback on their leadership styles and are then given a current organizational issue or problem to research or resolve. In the next 60 to 120 days, participants analyze the issues, develop recommendations, and present their findings to the organization's executive team. The use of this action-learning technique has proved successful in helping the organization find solutions to longstanding problems, as well as give participants the opportunity to experience the inherent ambiguity in their roles and to learn that executive-level problems often have more than one correct solution.

Alignment with Talent-Management Systems

Although it is fair to say that talent-management systems and leadership-development programs are aligned, it is probably more accurate to say that business strategy drives talent management, which in turn drives leadership development. Though a subtle distinction, Washington Group believes that once it understands where it is going (strategy) and understands the available talent, it is possible to design development programs (as well as hiring strategies) to ensure that the right talent is in place.

The organization considers its top talent pool to comprise 8 to 10 percent of the workforce. This high-potential pool is identified and reviewed by business units and key functional areas (project management, finance, business development, etc.) and becomes part of the Washington Group Talent Bank (see Figure E.4). Special attention is paid to identifying potential future positions and then assessing the development needs required to ensure that the person is capable of performing in the new job.

Although formal succession planning is used at the business-unit level and above, the process of identifying people who are currently ready, or who will be in one to three years, to assume positions of more responsibility is finding its way to lower levels of the organization.

Although each business unit conducts its own internal talent re-

Figure E.4. Washington Group's talent-development process.

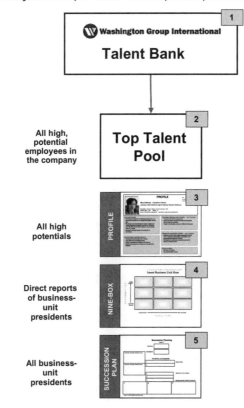

views with the office of the chairman twice a year, key organizational leaders come together once a year for a formal roll-up that looks at talent across the organization. These discussions often result in cross-business-unit assignments to ensure that high potentials are exposed to various segments of the business. The organization's board of directors also reviews key talent, especially those on succession plans for key executives.

Alignment with Career Transitions

Although Washington Group does not tie movement into a new position with specific training or development activities once individuals are in the positions, it works to ensure that people are ready—with the requisite knowledge and experience—prior to such moves. The process is both formal (through high-potential reviews, LEAP, etc.) and informal though coaching and mentoring. For example, stretch assignments frequently provide smooth transitions into new, formal job assignments. Because stretch assignments are just that—they place people slightly outside their comfort zones in order to encourage them to practice strategic agility, among other skills—they also include a safety net to ensure that the individuals don't fail.

Leadership-Development Approaches and Tools

Like most companies today, Washington Group faces the same potential shortage of qualified workers that was described as the "war for talent," in the 1990s.[1] As a means of minimizing that shortage and attracting the next generation of workers, the organization established a Professional Rotational Experience Project (PREP), a two-year program for recent college graduates. In PREP, highly screened, diverse participants are given three or four assignments within their disciplines. Although the early focus of the PREP has been to develop a base of project managers, it was expanded into other disciplines in late 2006. Because participants work in at least two different business units and with different leaders, they gain a unique perspective on the organization while honing their project-management skills.

Although the concept of a high potential is open to interpretation, when defined as "someone who has shown learning agility," the term becomes much clearer. Washington Group uses the concept of learning agility to help identify those who may be considered to have high potential and uses stretch assignments to test the validity of the label. In other words, if someone can step into an unfamiliar role and quickly muster the resources to be successful, it's likely that the person has the ability to assume positions of more or different responsibilities, thus fitting the definition of high potential.

As an example, a top finance and accounting individual went from the highest level in finance and accounting in one business unit to an operations position in another. It was a significant stretch for him, but he wanted operations experience to round out his business expertise. In another case, two chemical engineers were removed from their project-related work and tasked to develop the organization's college rotation program.

A recurring theme at Washington Group is the development of project-management talent—owing, in part, to the fact that managing projects is a large share of the organization's business portfolio. The organization actively focuses on standardizing its project-management approach under the term "The Washington Way," which emphasizes consistent, repeatable processes from its smallest to largest projects. The organization is affiliated with both the Construction Industry Institute, provider of best practices through research, related initiatives, and industry alliances, and the Project Management Institute, which provides training, benchmarking, and advice worldwide in the area of project management. Part of the project-development initiative will be to identify mastery-level skills that highly effective project managers possess, and then develop learning opportunities for those new to the function so that they can also acquire the skills.

Executive Support for Leadership Development

Washington Group's heritage organizations had decidedly divergent approaches to leadership development. But after emerging from financial restructuring in 2001, the organization assumed a planned, disciplined, and consistent stance on this topic, backed by strategy and tactics to realize the benefits of developing leaders. Leadership development is one of the organization's most important strategic initiatives and is vigorously supported by the senior leadership team.

Current leaders are used as coaches and mentors, and they are expected to take this responsibility seriously and as part of the way business is done in the organization. The organization offers classroom training on the topic of coaching and also has online resources available. This year, for the first time, "developing and coaching others" will become a standard job expectation for managers in the Development Planner.

The organization looks at leaders as both teachers and learners and routinely structures its formal development programs to include opportunities to assume both roles. In the Leaders Forum, for example, senior leaders take active roles in teaching topics during the course. They also spend two or more hours on the final day soliciting feedback about the organization and their leadership styles. Nearly every business review (held quarterly) includes an instructional component, and the yearly talent reviews almost always include outside speakers. On a more individual level, the organization encourages its managers to use the Development Planner as a tool to enhance their own growth by soliciting feedback from employees. In addition, managers often host or conduct "lunch and learn" sessions for their own staffs. These sessions are generally open to people from different areas within the organization to improve the learning experience.

Aligning coaching and mentoring with individual activities takes place, in a structured manner, through the Development Planner process and, in a less structured manner, during daily interactions with employees. Managers are encouraged to understand the professional goals of their staff and to help them find the right development means to achieve these. On the other hand, because employees are primarily responsible for their own growth and development, it is incumbent on them to solicit help from their manager. In a sense, this "checks and balances system" holds both managers and employees accountable to achieve organizational goals and to use these goals as a means of developing professionally.

Because the senior leaders at Washington Group are closely linked to leadership development, they usually find individually fulfilling ways to become involved in programs. In the Executive Roundtable, for example, senior leaders are asked to sponsor one of the sessions and, with a little coaching, select an action-learning topic of relevance to their function. The organization is less concerned about choosing *where* a senior leader might become involved and more concerned about *when* an opportunity becomes available. Put another way, nearly every leadership-development offering includes some form of senior leader involvement. To be more specific, when leadership-development programs are taken to major organizational locations, they consistently use the most senior leader to introduce the course and talk about organizational initiatives from his or her perspective. In other cases, the organization will ask a business-unit president to be part of a course offering at its corporate headquarters. Generally, course designers have a clear sense of the strengths of each senior leader and seek ways to capitalize on these strengths to the benefit of course participants.

High Potentials

High potentials are identified at Washington Group through a yearly talent-review process conducted at the business-unit level and then rolled up to the organization level. Those identified in this process become part of a "talent bank" (Figure E.4) that contains resumes and skills data on high-potential and other professional employees. The talent bank is an online, Web-based application containing the resumes, technical skills, and career interests of Washington Group employees. Those flagged in the talent bank as "top talent" show potential to move into more responsible or challenging assignments.

To date, about 1,200 employees are identified as top talent. Each employee's accomplishments are included as part of his or her profile. The profile serves as a means of engaging reviewers in a discussion of the individual and includes information on accomplishments from the previous year, development completed plus development planned, and potential future positions. Three of the components (accomplishments, development completed, and development planned) originate in the Development Planner and are modified, as needed, for use on the profile form. The nine-box performance-and-potential form is completed for the business-unit presidents and their direct reports. This visual representation of performance and potential serves as a discussion starter for the talent-review process. Succession planning is completed in conjunction with the talent review. This form is used by the business-unit presidents to identify their potential replacements as well as determine the replacements' readiness to assume the position. This process is also used at lower levels in the organization.

The subject of whether high potentials should be made aware of their status is one that stimulates discussion within the organization. In 2001, when high potentials were first identified, the practice was not to inform them of their status. At the time, many believed that the process should mature before openly communicating such potentially sensitive information. However, some senior executives have now begun to inform employees of their high-potential status with the caveat that, based on performance and other factors, it is possible to move in and out of the high-potential pool. The underlying debate of whether an employee is helped or hindered by knowing his or her status, and whether the organization is raising expectations beyond what it can reasonably deliver, remains undecided.

Washington Group does not communicate high-potential criteria to the organization as a whole. Instead, such criteria are clearly communicated to those involved in the talent-management and review process. The process, however, has evolved from the first use of the nine-box chart four years ago. Originally, only the terms "potential and performance" and "low to high" were used with the belief that managers would understand the concepts and draw conclusions, accurately placing individuals in the proper box. Clarifying definitions that describe observable behaviors have now been added to the nine boxes. In addition, the organization now uses additional descriptors and definitions such as "learning agility" and "strategic agility" as a means of more accurately selecting individuals who could be considered high potential.

Implementing the Successful Leadership-Development Strategy

During yearly strategic and business-planning sessions, employee development and leadership development are key discussion areas. The strategic-planning sessions take a broad view of economic issues that span multiple markets, trends in the industry, and Washington Group's own organizational performance. So, as the organization's strategic plan is updated, so is the employee-development strategic plan. The office of the chairman reviews and approves the plan as well as the financial commitments resulting from it.

Implementation of Leadership-Development Programs

For the most part, delivery of leadership-development programs is a process centralized at the corporate level—exceptions would be found in the organization's government-owned, contractor-operated facilities such as the Washington Group Savannah River Company where such training can be highly technical and often directed by customers. Cultural differences are addressed in various ways and the topic of "diversity in the largest sense of that word" (a phrase coined by one of the organization's executives to broaden the definition beyond the more typical categories of race and gender) is included in all leadership-development offerings. Expanding course offerings to more inclusively touch on international issues is under way, as is addressing language training. Cultural awareness is also being addressed through an innovative "life and culture" series available through the organization's online learning platform, making such training readily available to all employees regardless of location.

Development programs, by their very nature, nurture both strength and capacity as well as remediate weaknesses. When viewed from a high level, the organization's programs are designed primarily to build strength and capacity. In the case of individuals, however, some of these could be viewed as remediating weaknesses.

For the most part, development programs, including those related to e-learning platforms, are designed to meet the needs of individual learners, their development plans, and their roles in the organization. For example, the organization's first-line management course, called "Principles of Management," targets people who are new to a managerial role. Although it could be attended by those with management experience, it is tailored to the requirements of those with little or no experience. Washington Group, as it designs and develops courses, assesses the knowledge and skills needed by those considered "master performers," or who exemplify best practices in their fields. Exceptions to individually tailored development experiences include safety, ethics training, and general security training, which are standardized for all positions.

Program content is reviewed on an ongoing basis. Minor adjustments are made on the fly, based on participant feedback, although it is only done when the feedback is sufficient to justify changes. Overall content reviews are conducted during the employee-development's strategic-planning process.

Governance

One and one-half full-time equivalents are dedicated to leadership-development programs. There is no formal governing council for leadership development. Rather, this is a shared responsibility among stakeholders including the CEO and his staff, the integrated staffing and career-development function, human resources, and the organization's board of directors. (The board is knowledgeable and aware of the organization's programs but does not participate in the management of them.)

The organization does not formally track the time line executives invest in leadership development because it does not believe the means of doing so would yield a meaningful measure. Instead, it encourages its managers to invest a minimum of 15 to 20 percent of their time in people development. Because the organization is very broad in how "people development" is defined, the actual time is likely greater than that number. The organization does put 30 percent of an executive's pay "at risk," related to developing employees.

Executive Investment

Although the organization places strong emphasis on the involvement of its top executives, it is now working actively to push its leadership influence deeper into the organization. The office of the chairman remains heavily committed to the LEAP project, yet it now serves as an advocate for participants, sharing the mentoring with previous LEAP participants and other recognized senior, high-potential employees. The CEO stays involved in a shadowing program for these people. In what may be a unique twist, the office of the chairman does not hold "personal ownership" for high potentials; rather, it holds business-unit presidents and others responsible and accountable for this. Such delegation, in the minds of the executives, is modeling the principle of empowerment and the fundamental belief that all leaders are responsible for developing people—not just those at the top.

Evaluating Success

Washington Group President Steve Hanks says that, when it comes to metrics, he doesn't want people "getting too caught up in statistics." Yet, he attributes the organization's strong financial performance directly to its focus on developing people. Since 2002, the organization's net income per employee has jumped 60 percent, and it is exceeding its goal of 10 percent compound annual growth. Notwithstanding Hanks's counsel about metrics, the organization takes certain measures seriously—especially those related to its ability to attract, develop, and retain employees. Because the organization uses its "developing people" proposition to attract new employees, it closely monitors the ratios between applications, interviews, and hires among others, and uses these data to determine how effectively it is attracting top talent. The organization also scrutinizes the development of its high-potential pool by tracking completed development activities, job progression, and retention. These metrics are reviewed during the annual talent reviews. Participants in certain programs, including LEAP, the Leaders Forum, and the Executive Roundtable, are consistently surveyed for feedback on the programs' effectiveness.

Data from these measures are factored into the organization's leadership strategy, although they are more frequently used to make midcourse corrections or small changes to the approach than to significantly reshape programs. Washington Group does not attempt to directly link individual outcomes from its leadership programs with organizational performance, believing that there are far too many factors involved to establish a causal relationship. It does, however, through its development-planning process, translate organization-wide business objectives into working-group goals and objectives. These, in turn, are tied to individual performance expectations and are measured and discussed during the annual Development Planner review cycle conducted by managers and employees.

Communicating Success

Because Washington Group actively engages its management team in the development process, it uses them to communicate program expectations and success. They (and employees) are provided organization publications, such as *The Washington Way*, that routinely feature articles on employee development. *The Leader's Edge* is a publication for managers that features development ideas and is also used for this purpose. Organization-wide meetings, held at major locations, feature organization and local executives who speak to professional development among other topics.

Assessing for the Future

Future leadership development needs are determined in multiple ways, many of which were covered in this case study. In addition, the employee-development staff routinely solicits feedback from managers and employees when it meets with them on other subjects. Portions of the Leaders Forum and the Executive Roundtable are set aside for candid discussions on leadership needs. One of the more revealing—and quantifiable—ways the organization designs and shapes leadership-development programs is through the aggregated results of 360-degree assessments. For example, using a large sample of 360-degree feedback from high potentials, the organization designed its Executive Roundtable to expose participants to executive-level decision making in a real-life environment.

Innovative Aspects

Several features of Washington Group's approach have proved successful for the organization and may have value to others. They include:

▲ High level of executive engagement

▲ Use of senior leaders as instructors

▲ Linking executive compensation to leadership development

▲ Use of alternative teaching methods, such as using movies, as a way to show effective leadership behaviors

▲ Cultural assessments conducted by course participants

▲ Theme-based training that teaches leadership concepts through the use of analogies (Executive Roundtable)

▲ Using participants as teachers (Leaders Forum)

▲ Shadowing senior executives

Critical Success Factors and Lessons Learned

Because Washington Group is a melding of a number of heritage organizations, its approach to developing leaders was unique to all. The success of its leadership initiatives is due, in part, to focusing on common strengths rather than a dissection-through-discussion of its weaknesses. Put another way, its leadership strategies focus on where the organization wants its leaders to be in the future rather than what has not worked in the past. In the Leaders Forum, for example, a closing case study asks participants to advise each other on what they can do to be better communicators. This "don't throw the problem over the transom" approach encourages individuals to accept responsibility for making change in their own leadership styles. Another success factor is the senior leadership's involvement in course content. Generally, the design team interviews key stakeholders, evaluates their recommendations, and incorporates these during the development process.

Under the category of lessons learned are the following:

▲ *Use lessons learned to build teamwork and solve problems.* Significant issues surfaced following the first round of succession planning. A formal lessons-learned conducted with the senior staff identified these and resolved them for following years.

▲ *Overcommunicate, especially when introducing new programs or making changes to existing ones.* Implementing new programs can stress individuals who are otherwise occupied with routine work. Assuming these people will be on board with the changes proved to be a bad assumption. The organization used online meetings, teleconferences, and one-on-one meetings to improve communication and to ensure the success of new programs.

▲ *Don't position "training" as the way to develop people.* Perhaps it is human nature to assume that training is the answer to performance problems or the way to develop additional skills and knowledge. Research shows otherwise. As a result, the organization leadership constantly challenges managers to think much more broadly on how to develop people.

▲ *Consider financial incentives to solve tough issues.* Washington Group learned early on that it could benefit from improved intra-business-unit cooperation. Although not a unique problem, significant progress occurred when part of an executive's incentive pay was put at risk.

▲ *Don't assume that senior leaders are on the same page when it comes to the importance of developing leaders.* Although Washington Group senior leaders agreed that developing leaders is a critical ingredient in the organization's sustainable success, they did not agree on who should be developed and at what level this should occur. The solution occurred as the employee-development team took a blended approach that offered elements to address all viewpoints. The resulting programs were strengthened, not weakened, by this.

Notes

Chapter 1. What We Have Learned About Strategic Leadership Development

1. Paul Bernthal and Richard S. Wellins, *Leadership Forecast: 2003–2004* (Bridgeville, PA: Development Dimensions International, Inc., 2004).

2. Michelle Salob and Shelli Greenslade, "How the Top 20 Companies Grow Great Leaders" (Hewitt Associates, 2005). http://www.hewittassociates.com/_MetaBas icCMAssetCache_/Assets/Articles/top_companies_2005.pdf. Accessed June 2007.

3. "Sixth Annual Benchmarking Report" (Corporate University Xchange, 2004). http://www.corpu.com. Accessed June 2007.

4. James Bolt, *Executive Development Trends 2000* (Kansas City, MO: Executive Development Associates, Inc., 2000); James Bolt, *Executive Development Trends 2004: Filling the Talent Gap* (Kansas City, MO: Executive Development Associates, Inc., 2004).

5. Bolt, *Executive Development Trends 2004: Filling the Talent Gap.*

6. Salob and Greenslade, "How the Top 20 Companies Grow Great Leaders."

7. Bernthal and Wellins, *Leadership Forecast: 2003–2004*; Sheila M. Rioux and Paul Bernthal, *Succession Management Practices* (Bridgeville, PA: Development Dimensions International, 2006).

8. Scott Saslow, *Leadership Development in European Organisations: Challenges and Best Practices* (Palo Alto, CA: The Danish Leadership Institute and Institute of Executive Development, 2004).

9. Donald L. Kirkpatrick, *Evaluating Training Programs: The Four Levels*, 3rd ed. (San Francisco: Berrett-Koehler, 2005); Jack J. Phillips, *Return on Investment in Training and Performance Improvement Programs*, 2nd ed. (Burlington, MA: Butterworth-Heinemann, 2003).

Chapter 3. Building an Aligned Architecture for Strategic Leadership Development

1. Michael M. Lombardo and Robert W. Eichinger, *The Leadership Machine: Architecture to Develop Leaders for Any Future*, 3rd ed. (Minneapolis: Lominger Ltd, 2000).

Chapter 4. Implementing Successful Strategic Leadership Development

1. Robert M. Fulmer and Marshall Goldsmith, *The Leadership Investment: How the World's Best Organizations Gain Strategic Advantage Through Leadership Development* (New York: AMACOM, 2000).

Chapter 5. Leveraging Leadership Development for High Potentials

1. Steve A. Stumpf, The Fred J. Springer chair in Business Leadership and Professor of Management at the Villanova School of Business made significant contributions to this chapter.
2. Paul Bernthal and Richard S. Wellins, *Leadership Forecast: 2003–2004* (Bridgeville, PA: Development Dimensions International, Inc., 2004).
3. Michelle Salob and Shelli Greenslade, "How the Top 20 Companies Grow Great Leaders" (Hewitt Associates, 2005). http://www.hewittassociates.com/_MetaBasicCMAssetCache_/Assets/Articles/top_companies_2005.pdf. Accessed June 2007.
4. Bernthal and Wellins, *Leadership Forecast: 2003–2004*.
5. Robert M. Fulmer, Marshall Goldsmith, and Sumeet Varghese, "Do You Know Who Your Next CEO Is?" (Washington, D.C.: Human Capital Institute, 2006).
6. Robert M. Fulmer, Philip A. Gibbs, and Marshall Goldsmith, "Developing Leaders: How Winning Companies Keep on Winning," *Sloan Management Review* 41, no. 1, pp. 49–59 (2000).
7. Fulmer, Goldsmith, and Varghese, "Do You Know."
8. Fulmer, Goldsmith, and Varghese, "Do You Know."
9. Bernthal and Wellins, *Leadership Forecast: 2003–2004*.
10. Fulmer, Goldsmith, and Varghese, "Do You Know."
11. Jonathan P. Doh and Stephen A. Stumpf, eds., *Handbook on Responsible Leadership and Governance in Global Business* (Cheltenham, UK: Edward Elgar, 2005); J. J. McCall, "Leadership and Ethics: Corporate Accountability to Whom, for What, and by What Means," *Journal of Business Ethics* 38, no. 1 (2002).
12. Fulmer, Goldsmith, and Varghese, "Do You Know."

Chapter 6. Evaluating Success in Strategic Leadership Development

1. Kate Charlton, *Executive Education: Evaluating the Return on Investment, Findings from the US: An Appendix to the May 2005 Report* (Hertfordshire, UK: Ashridge/UNICON, 2005).

2. Jack J. Phillips, *Return on Investment in Training and Performance Improvement Programs,* 2nd ed. (Burlington, MA: Butterworth-Heinemann, 2003); Donald L. Kirkpatrick, *Evaluating Training Programs: The Four Levels,* 3rd ed. (San Francisco: Berrett-Koehler, 2005).

3. "Sixth Annual Benchmarking Report" (Corporate University Xchange, 2004). http://www.corpu.com. Accessed June 2007.

4. Tammy Galvin, "The 2004 Top 100," *Training* magazine, April 1, 2004. Available from www.trainingmag.com.

5. Kirkpatrick, *Evaluating Training Programs.*

6. Robert O. Brinkerhoff, *The Success Case Method: Find Out Quickly What's Working and What's Not* (San Francisco: Berrett-Koehler, 2003).

7. Brinkerhoff, *Success Case Method.* The success case method developed by Robert O. Brinkerhoff is a quick and simple process that combines analysis of extreme groups with case study and storytelling. The essential purpose of a success case study is to find out how well some organizational initiative (e.g., a training program, a new work method) is working. A success case study also identifies and explains the contextual factors that differentiate successful from unsuccessful adopters of new initiatives.

8. Tezeta Tulloch, "The Success Case Method: Finding out What Works," *The Evaluation Exchange* 9, no. 4 (2003).

Washington Group International

1. Ed Michaels, Helen Handfield-Jones, and Beth Axelrod. *The War for Talent* (Boston: Harvard Business School Press, 2001).

References

Bartlett, Christopher, A., and Andrew N. McLean. *GE's Talent Machine: The Making of a CEO*. Boston: Harvard Business School, 2003.

Bernthal, Paul, and Richard S. Wellins. *Leadership Forecast: 2003–2004*. Bridgeville, PA: Development Dimensions International, Inc., 2004.

Bolt, James. *Executive Development Trends 2000*. Kansas City, MO: Executive Development Associates, Inc., 2000.

———. *Executive Development Trends 2004: Filling the Talent Gap*. Kansas City, MO: Executive Development Associates, Inc., 2004.

Brinkerhoff, Robert O. *The Success Case Method: Find Out Quickly What's Working and What's Not*. San Francisco: Berrett-Koehler, 2003.

Charlton, Kate. *Executive Education: Evaluating the Return on Investment, Bringing the Client Voice into the Debate*. Hertfordshire, UK: Ashridge/UNICON, 2005.

———. *Executive Education: Evaluating the Return on Investment, Findings from the US: An Appendix to the May 2005 Report*. Hertfordshire, UK: Ashridge, 2006.

Corporate Leadership Council. *Driving Performance and Retention Through Employee Engagement*. Washington, D.C.: Corporate Leadership Council/Corporate Executive Board, 2004.

Corporate Leadership Council. *Realizing the Potential of Rising Talent Survey, Volume 1*. Washington, D.C.: Corporate Leadership Council, 2005.

Corporate University Xchange. *Sixth Annual Benchmarking Report*. Harrisburg, PA: Corporate University Xchange, 2004.

Doh, Jonathan P., and Stephen A. Stumpf, eds. *Handbook on Responsible Leadership and Governance in Global Business*. Cheltenham, UK: Edward Elgar, 2005.

Duke Corporate Education. *Creating a Leadership Architecture*. Durham, NC: Duke Corporate Education, 2005.

Fulmer, Robert M. *Next Generation HR Practices*. Houston, TX: American Productivity and Quality Center, 2005.

———. *Strategic Human Resource Development*. Houston, TX: American Productivity and Quality Center, 2006.

Fulmer, Robert M., and Jay A. Conger. *Growing Your Company's Leaders: How Great Organizations Use Succession Management to Sustain Competitive Advantage*. New York: AMACOM, 2004.

Fulmer, Robert M., Philip A. Gibbs, and Marshall Goldsmith. "Developing Leaders: How Winning Companies Keep on Winning." *Sloan Management Review* 41, no. 1 (2000), pp. 49–59.

Fulmer, Robert M., and Marshall Goldsmith. *The Leadership Investment: How the World's Best Organizations Gain Strategic Advantage Through Leadership Development*. New York: AMACOM, 2000.

Fulmer, Robert M., Marshall Goldsmith, and Sumeet Varghese. "Do You Know Who Your Next CEO Is?" Washington, D.C.: Human Capital Institute, 2006.

Galvin, Tammy. "The 2004 Top 100." *Training* magazine, April 1, 2004. Available from www.trainingmag.com.

Kirkpatrick, Donald L. *Evaluating Training Programs: The Four Levels*. 3rd ed. San Francisco: Berrett-Koehler, 2005.

Lombardo, Michael M., and Robert W. Eichinger. *The Leadership Machine: Architecture to Develop Leaders for Any Future*, 3rd ed. Minneapolis: Lominger Ltd, 2000.

McCall, J. J. "Leadership and Ethics: Corporate Accountability to Whom, for What, and by What Means." *Journal of Business Ethics* 38, no.1 (2002), pp. 133–39.

Phillips, Jack J. *Return on Investment in Training and Performance Improvement Programs*, 2nd ed. Burlington, MA: Butterworth-Heinemann, 2003.

Ready, Douglas A. "How to Grow Great Leaders." *Harvard Business Review*, December 2004, pp. 93–100.

Rioux, Sheila M., and Paul Bernthal. *Succession Management Practices*. Bridgeville, PA: Development Dimensions International, 2006.

Salob, Michelle, and Shelli Greenslade. "How the Top 20 Companies Grow Great Leaders." Hewitt Associates, 2005. http://www.hewittassociates.com/_MetaBasicCMAssetCache_/Assets/Articles/top_companies_2005.pdf. Accessed June 2007.

Saslow, Scott. *Current Challenges in Leadership Development*. Palo Alto, CA: Institute of Executive Development, 2004.

———. *Leadership Development in European Organisations: Challenges and Best Practices*. Palo Alto, CA: The Danish Leadership Institute and Institute of Executive Development, 2004.

———. "Transforming Corporate Leadership: Best Practices in Executive Education." Palo Alto, CA: Institute of Executive Development, 2004.

"Sixth Annual Benchmarking Report." Corporate University Xchange, 2004. http://www.corpu.com. Accessed June 2007.

Stumpf, Stephen A. "Development of the Relationship Management Survey: A Tool for Assessing Performance and Career Success of Professional Service Professionals." *Journal of Organizational Culture, Communication, and Conflict* 11, no. 1 (2007), pp. 203–225.

Tulloch, Tezeta. "The Success Case Method: Finding out What Works." *The Evaluation Exchange* 9, no. 4 (2003). http://www.gse.harvard.edu/hfrp/eval/issue24/book_review.html. Accessed June 2007.

Index